I0817481

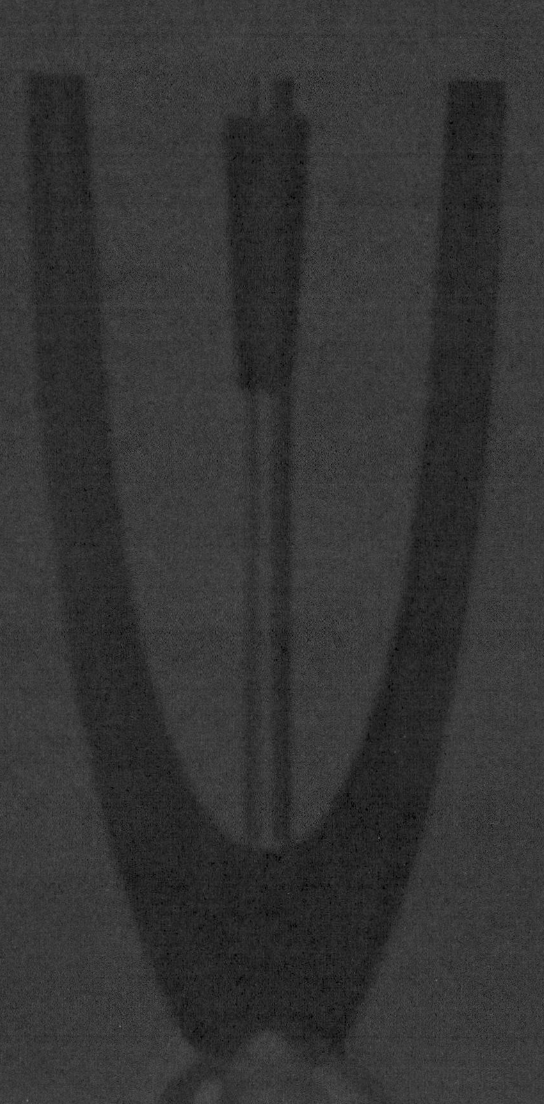

MODELINE OF CALIFORNIA

PIONEER OF MODERN LIGHTING

Nick Ferrell

SCHIFFER PUBLISHING

4880 Lower Valley Road • Atglen, PA 19310

Library of Congress Control Number: 2025930181

Designed by Danielle D. Farmer
Type set in Scandia

ISBN: 978-0-7643-7028-1
ePub: 978-1-5073-0615-4

Printed in China

Published by Schiffer Publishing, Ltd.
4880 Lower Valley Road
Atglen, PA 19310
Phone: (610) 593-1777; Fax: (610) 593-2002
Email: info@schifferbooks.com
Web: www.schifferbooks.com

Contents

Introduction

Modeline (pronounced: Model-Line) of California is widely considered the most innovative and influential American lighting manufacturer of the mid-twentieth century. It takes only a cursory examination of their charming wooden lamps to succumb entirely to their spell and see how this designation not only is justified but perhaps does not go far enough in recognizing the importance of this long-defunct luxury lamp firm. From the economic uncertainty of the postwar years, into the glamor of 1950s Hollywood, and all the way through to America's winning of the space race, Modeline of California did more than merely ride the train of modernism—it powered the engine and created the style that became the essence of modern design in lighting. Owned and operated by Bernie and Esther Roberts, Modeline of California was founded on three general ideas: that interior lighting ought to be coordinated with the furniture in a home, that interior lighting should be an extension of one's tastes and personality, and that only wood could serve as a suitable material to endure the ceaselessly changing preferences of American consumers. These ideas proved to resonate so successfully with buyers that the eyes of the entire lighting industry turned to Modeline. Shortly after Modeline's initial success, several lighting firms outfitted their entire operation with the necessary tooling to replicate the Modeline style. Other firms were founded entirely to do the same thing. Modeline lamps and the Modeline style burst quickly and monumentally into American homes, spreading from Los Angeles to Manhattan with the intensity of a California wildfire. For a time, one could hardly open the Sunday paper or turn on the television without seeing these wonderful wooden lamps. Being the life's work and passion of the Robertses, the narrative history of this brand is indistinguishable from the stories of their personal lives. Bernie and Esther's philosophical ideology permeated Modeline. The Jewish concept of tikkun olam informed all decisions made at Modeline of California. This idea—that individuals are responsible not only for their own moral and ethical behavior, but that they assume partial responsibility for the restoration of the world to spiritual principles—defined the soul of the company. What this meant to Bernie and Esther in the context of mid-1940s American culture was that the skill of an individual would be the sole determining factor in their hiring. To the best of their ability, no consideration was given to such factors as race, sex, ethnicity, nationality, religious preference, or political affiliation. Bernie and Esther were committed to the respect of the personhood and dignity of each individual worker at the firm. Unencumbered by factors that too often limited the decisions made by their contemporaries, Modeline of California was free to secure the most-talented designers in the world. Arthur Jacobs, Jack Haywood, John Keal, Bill Dorff, Martin Aakervik, Ben Gurule, Lynn Lawrence, Byron Botker, Mark Stehrenberger, Charles Gibilterra, Heinz Meier, and many others created a powerhouse of design. In Modeline's thirty-five years of existence, the firm contributed over four thousand unique atomic, modern, and space-age lamp designs to homes of the twentieth century. So how did the history of Modeline, this once-great California lamp company, become nearly completely lost? The primary purpose of this book is to tell that history so that it cannot be lost again.

Soon after I founded my company, Esthetic Vintage, and began restoring and selling twentieth-century designer lighting, the industry quickly introduced me to Modeline products. The first Modeline lamp I bought left an indelible mark on me. I fell under the seductive effects of this lamp. The design, pulling inspiration from elements in nature, was perfectly tasteful and elegant. The construction of finely sculpted wood carved into impossibly delicate forms was superior to the capabilities of any other lamp manufacturer at the time and most still to this day. Even the act of turning the lamp on was special—activated by the pressing of a saucer-shaped wooden detail. Modeline was in a class of its own. This sentiment was not unique, judging by the response of the market to my initial offering of Modeline lamps for sale. Early in my dealing of these lamps, I witnessed two women at an estate sale in southern Michigan engage in a physical altercation while both were attempting to purchase the same Modeline lamp. While that could have been reduced to greed, explaining their impassioned moment away by their desire to make a profit, similar outbursts of emotion are not rare even among retail buyers. Customers of mine have offered vehicles, Rolex watches, and other fine jewelry in exchange for these lamps. I have sold these lamps to clients in Australia, Japan, and the United Arab Emirates only to have them spend additional thousands of dollars to have the lamps delivered to them. There is something undeniably enchanting about Modeline of California. There is an ink pen, and there is Montblanc. There is a sedan, and there is Rolls Royce. There is a table lamp, and there is Modeline of California. Among the countless thousands of mid-twentieth-century modern lamp designs and companies, assuming that buyers always vote with the dollar, Modeline is the undisputed champion.

Modeline's sculptural wooden forms are thin and delicate in relation to their often-gargantuan size. When one first sees a Modeline lamp, it is typical to wonder, "How is that standing?" They command attention not only for their ostensibly impossible stature but also for the design's obvious genius. The warm earth tones of a rich walnut finish contrasting against brilliantly polished brass hardware emit unadulterated sophistication. Activating a Modeline lamp allows one to participate more deeply in this sense of wonder. Upon depressing the aforementioned wooden pull switch that Modeline often employed in its designs, one is greeted with a pleasant, baritone click—not the crunch or snap typical of lamp lighting. It is like winding a top-quality watch or starting a luxurious automobile. Even the most inexperienced lighting novice will recognize immediately and involuntarily that this product is different in kind from all others.

After purchasing my third or fourth Modeline lamp, I did what any curious person who grew up in the age of information would do—I asked Google all the relevant questions. I wanted to know everything that the world knew about this brand. How did it begin? Which designers were behind it? How did they so effectively outperform their peers? My disappointment grew with each successive search finding nothing remotely authoritative or reliable. Worse yet, much of the information available was demonstrably untrue. Desperate to find something, I asked several of the more established dealers what they knew about the brand. The few who replied gave me the same points that were bouncing around the internet. "It was a California lamp company that was founded in 1957, and they made lamps out of teak and some of them were designed by Adrian Pearsall and Milo Baughman." I was not new to twentieth-century lighting, so I knew that at least most of this information—save the California bit—was incorrect. Despite feeling overwhelmed and ill-equipped to take on a research project of such an apparently large scale, I was taken by a certain element of excitement. Growing up in the Google age also came with its disadvantages. For people like me who are most deeply engaged in life when faced with some degree of mystery, the idea that all information is available to one who simply asks the correct questions on the internet can be a disheartening one. I made Modeline my obsession.

I kick-started my research in California newspaper archives. I flipped through thousands of pages in a wasteland of classifieds and dating advice until I found an ad. "Wonderful Wood Lamps by Modeline of California," they often exclaimed while displaying the brand's top sellers. I scanned and saved these ads, then dated and organized them into folders. Many of these ads repeated the same information, but some of them offered the next clue—an address, a phone number, and sometimes the name of a designer. These clues provided me with more search queries, and I slowly built a timeline of models and designers. Next, I attempted to trace the genealogy of any designers or executives who were associated with Modeline. This process continued for more than a year. I became fully immersed in solving the Modeline mystery. I nervously dialed dozens of phone numbers. Most of these conversations were short. "My name is Nick Ferrell, and I'm in the process of researching an old lamp manufacturer. Does Modeline of California mean anything to you?" I was unprepared when I finally heard, "Yes, my father worked for Modeline." My anxious exhilaration eclipsed my ability to perceive that, in many cases, the individual on the other end of the telephone was far more caught off guard than I was. Most of these introductory conversations served the purpose only of scheduling a long-form conversation, which led to more names, places, dates, and stories. I began honing this craft and feeling more confident. The question that nobody would be able to answer was possibly the most relevant one—is there anything worth remembering about Modeline beside the lamps they left behind? Could I be burning energy on a painfully boring story? After hundreds of hours of conversations with individuals who were closely related to Modeline of California, I laid each story out in chronological order. A narrative finally emerged from this amalgamation of documents, photos, and oral history. Much to my relief, this story was as unusual, alluring, and wholly captivating as the charming wooden lamps themselves. I have done my best to do justice to this story and give the individuals behind Modeline of California their due. I hope you find this as fascinating as I have.

Courtesy of Jeff Jacobs

CHAPTER 1

A Million-Dollar Idea

Hollywood Black Friday. *Courtesy of the* Los Angeles Times *Photographic Archive, UCLA Library Special Collections*

The history of Modeline begins with an event that sent shockwaves of class warfare through postwar Hollywood. On October 5, 1945, seven months into a set decorators' strike at Warner Brothers Studios in Burbank, California, tensions reached a fever pitch when nonstriking employees attempted to pass the picketers to begin their workday. These frustrated picketers, likely dealing with heat exhaustion, failed to maintain what so far had been a nonviolent strike. The workers' cars were stopped by the crowd. When these workers failed to comply with the order not to cross the picket line, violence erupted and several of these cars were overturned. This quickly broke into a street brawl that demanded the immediate intervention of law enforcement. The police presence did little to quell the rapidly escalating fight. Batons, tear gas bombs, fire hoses, battery cables, chains, and all manners of improvised weapons were drawn in a street fight all too fit for Hollywood. This clash, dubbed Hollywood Black Friday by the local papers, would ultimately lead to the passage of the Taft-Hartley Act in 1947 and the breakup of the Conference of Studio Unions.

Of the four hundred arrests made that day, there was one individual jailed who had been a thorn in his union's side for quite some time—Emil Freed. Mr. Freed was a machinist by day and an activist by night. He had been instrumental in staging several protests in Los Angeles. He also spent his free time traveling from

California to Southern states to protest unfair convictions of Black citizens during the Jim Crow era. In the months that followed the end of World War II, fears of the spread of communism had saturated the American zeitgeist. Government officials employed dramatic tactics to stomp out Marxist leanings wherever they could be found. Even many of the unions were distancing themselves from the principles upon which they had been founded. Organizations had been established whose sole purpose was to investigate anyone who was suspected of embracing and proselytizing ideas that were "too far left." Freed's outspoken criticism of these institutions and his charismatic fashion of rallying others behind progressive causes earned him fierce loyalty among like-minded individuals, and unrelenting condemnation from his foes. This influence spread all the way to Lucile Ball, who was eventually questioned about her connection to Emil Freed by the Council on Un-American Activities. Freed's involvement in the Hollywood Black Friday riot finally gave authorities enough rope to hang him and his closest supporters. In addition to the charges of inciting a riot, which were brought on October 5, Freed was charged with failure to obey a court order, disturbing the peace, and refusal to disperse. Adding insult to injury, in an unprecedented tangle of union suspensions, charges of communism were issued on December 1, 1945, against Freed and seven of his most outspoken supporters in the International Association of Machinists Lodge 311. In addition to Freed, the seven men against whom these charges were brought were Al Sherman, Edward Fromson, Louis Baron, Jerome Kaye, Clair Killen, George Rapport, and, as relevant to Modeline—Bernie Roberts.

Bernie, Esther, and Shirley Roberts, 1946.
Courtesy of Randi Måvestrand

Bernie Roberts was a thirty-seven-year-old former Brooklynite who had made his way to California at the age of sixteen to pursue a life far removed from his impoverished upbringing. Twenty-one years of attempts at attaining the American dream had instilled in him a loyalty to the working class and a deep suspicion of bosses. What was once a young man with dreams of carving out a place for himself in the world through hard work and determination was now a disillusioned and unemployed nearly forty-year-old with a wife and daughter. Being publicly branded with the scarlet letter of communism did not necessarily make Bernie unemployable, but it didn't help his prospects of finding work in the postwar era. Bernie was a skilled machinist who, until his union expulsion, had been working a wartime job fabricating aircraft parts for the defense industry. His intention had been to seek permanent employment through his union, but the recent expulsion eliminated this possibility. This turn toward a dismal financial outlook sent Bernie to seek assistance from a friend—Percy Solotoy.

Bernie and Percy had met in 1944, when Bernie performed several toolmaking projects for Solotoy's furniture-manufacturing firm Brown-Saltman. Since then, the two had become close friends. As a former lawyer and a successful furniture executive, Percy's opinions, particularly as they related to one's career decisions, carried considerable weight to Bernie. He viewed Percy as a mentor. When the opportunity arose at a party on New Year's Day 1946 for Bernie to seek Percy's advice, he seized it eagerly. Bernie confessed that his financial outlook was bleak, and that he had no clear idea on what to do. He was virtually blacklisted from any Los Angeles–area machining jobs, and he hadn't developed any other marketable skills. He went on to express concerns for the well-being of his wife and his daughter. Bernie was, in the most obvious possible fashion, stopping just short of fully swallowing his pride to ask Percy for a job. Percy mulled over what Bernie had said, and, as any good mentor might, gave Bernie the advice that he had not yet realized he needed. Percy talked about the new trends in furniture design and the growing demand for sculptural European- and Asian-influenced pieces. He remarked that buyers were struggling to find lamps that could be coordinated with modern furniture. The lighting industry was out of touch with consumers, offering only florid and ostentatious pieces from a bygone era. Percy believed that the creation of a modern lighting firm could be a million-dollar idea, and one that he would be happy to help promote. Bernie had nothing to lose and felt that a dramatic change was necessary to achieve the dreams that had once led him to pursue a better life in the Golden State. Bernie committed to starting such a lighting firm right on the spot.

Building this company would prove to be a difficult task. The cost of originality is having to forge one's own path, and this million-dollar idea would not be worth a penny if it could not be achieved practically. Bernie was not the first man to dream of founding a revolutionary firm. A particularly creative individual may conceive four or five such ideas before he is finished with his morning coffee. Bernie's first hurdle in creating this lamp company, though, would be his pride. He was fortunate to have the trust and friendship of his brother-in-law Carl Naftal. Carl was quite a successful businessman himself, owning and operating the women's dress company Carl Naftal Originals as well as owning and managing property throughout downtown Los Angeles. Bernie and Esther pitched this business to Carl and asked for his financial backing, to which Carl agreed.

Carl Naftal and Bernie Roberts. *Courtesy of Randi Måvestrand*

Next was the task of naming this new firm. Bernie and Esther ran through a long list of possibilities but did not fall in love with any of them until Esther proposed the idea of leaning on the power of association. This lamp company would be selling a product that the American consumer had not yet seen, and to which they had very little to compare. Since this company would design sculptural-wood lighting to coordinate with modern furniture, Esther suggested that they use some variation of the name of a sculpting clay that she had used as a child: Modeline. This name evoked feelings of nostalgia and creativity, and thoughts of sculptural forms in the minds of all who heard it.

Armed with a brand name and a loan of $7,000 from Carl, Bernie and Esther rented a 5,000-square-foot warehouse at 1009 Diamond Street in downtown Los Angeles. Bernie then secured the help of two fellow expelled union members, Clair Killen and George Rapport, to outfit the new plant with tooling. Bernie, George, and Clair fabricated their own tools to create high-quality sculptural lamps after realizing that the type of tooling needed was either unavailable or prohibitively expensive. For the first several months at Modeline, these men fabricated lathes, router tables, hydraulic presses, and specialty jigs. The rough designs that Bernie had drawn out for the first run of lamps required tooling far more precise than anything available in the case goods industry. Tolerances of 0.0050 inch allowed zero room for sloppy work. Still, if tooling alone was Modeline's obstacle, the firm may well have been off to a racing start. Hiring a small factory staff proved to be nearly impossible. Bernie sought out talented and experienced furniture builders, all of whom found themselves at a total loss when attempting to construct wooden lamps. Countless hours of experimentation and destroyed materials slowly began to bear fruit. By the end of 1946 the Diamond Street plant had a factory staff of five well-trained workers. The office responsibilities and executive functions were handled by Bernie and Esther with some help from their daughter, Shirley. In December 1946, with an excitement and confidence that was quite likely premature, Bernie wrote and submitted for newspaper publication a sentence that advertised a series of new lamps that had existed outside his imagination for only less than a month: 1009 Diamond Street—Wood Lamps by Modeline of California.

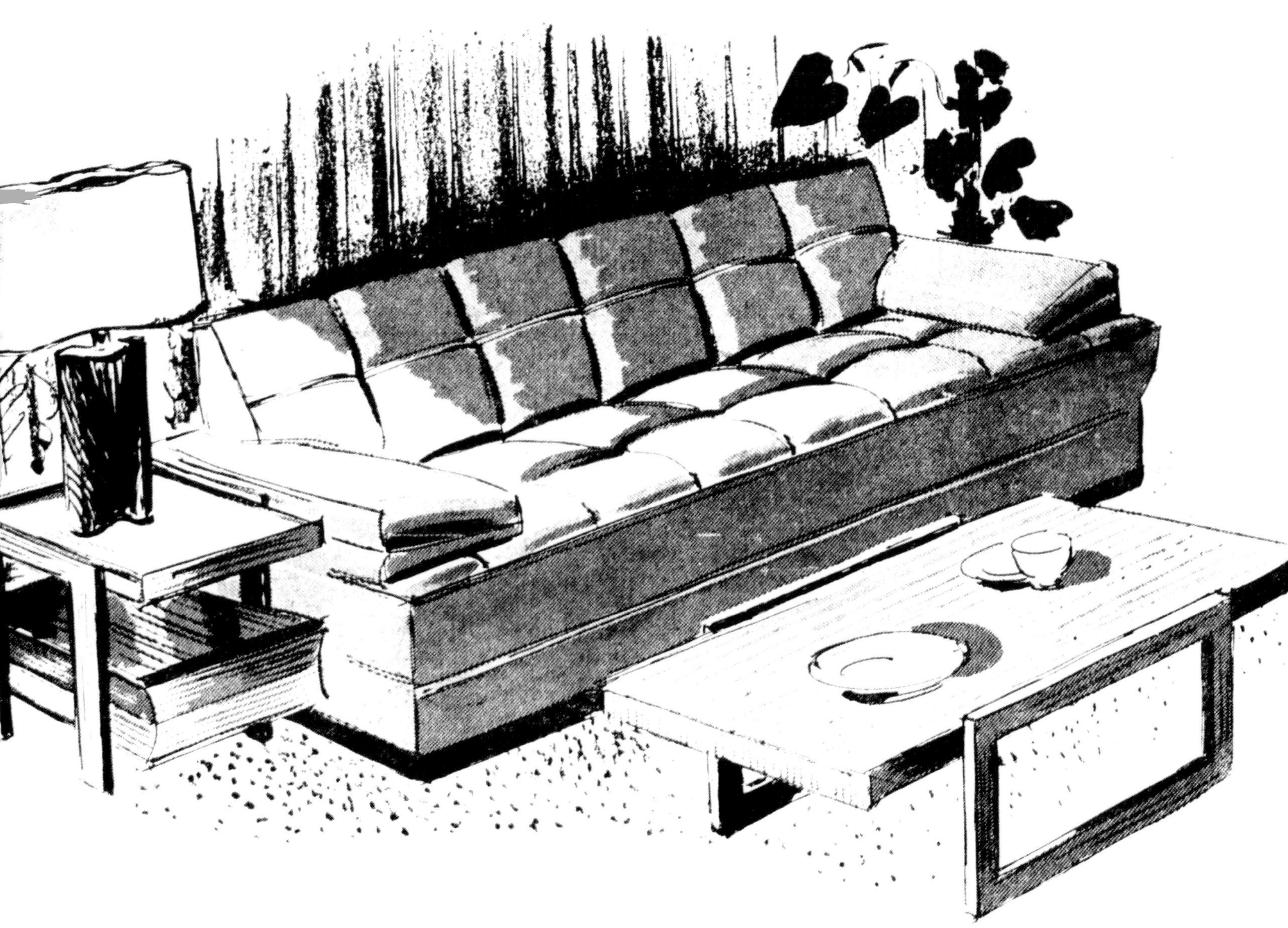

A 1949 advertisement pairing a Brown-Saltman sofa with a Modeline table lamp. *Copyright Modeline Co.*

Sculptured Lamps by MODELINE
OF CALIFORNIA

This product represents the exclusive design and craftsmanship of Modeline of California. It is made from the finest select hardwood, worked to exact design specifications.

Modern as tomorrow, every lamp in our collection is available in many colorings, multi-lacquered for smoothness and harmony; with shades to harmonize with the most 'difficult' rooms.

MEMBER • CALIFORNIA HOME FASHIONS

CHAPTER 2

Lynn Lawrence

Woefully, Modeline's first run of lamps could not have been less impressive. Elegant in their own way, but prosaic and unoriginal. Bent-wire forms with small ash wood accents made up the three initial offerings at Modeline. Not only was this design within the capabilities of any other lamp firm, but it may well have been mistaken for the handiwork of any budget company at the time. Aside from a bright-yellow "Modeline Company of California" sticker, these initial designs featured nothing new or revolutionary. Without an impressive offering to show, Bernie took on the task of developing a lampshade that would catch the eye of buyers and offer superior light diffusion. After some material and technique experimentation, he developed a method of thinning and applying an adhesive to fiberglass mat in a way that it could be formed to hold nearly any shape while maintaining its light-diffusing properties. He called this new shade material "Sofglo." Bernie took his process to an Echo Park fiberglass worker, Stew Benson. Stew agreed to make and supply these shades in large quantities for Modeline. These shades, when paired with the bent-wire bases, created an overall cohesive and distinctly atomic finished product. However, they still missed the mark in terms of offering a genuinely impressive and unique lamp. The expenses of operation, though, would not wait for the Modeline staff to be entirely pleased with their product line. The cash on hand at the firm was running low, so Bernie wasted no time in seeking dealers who were willing to carry this new product from Modeline. He loaded these wire lamps into his car and drove around an 80-mile radius of Los Angeles with Esther and Shirley. They stopped at every furniture store along the way, trying to sell the shop managers and owners on the merits of the new line of lamps by Modeline. Percy Solotoy assisted in phoning these shop owners to encourage them to carry these lamps. Ultimately, the Roberts family came back to the Modeline plant with good news—the first Modeline lamps would be available in thirteen Southern California furniture stores in January 1947.

Early sales showed some promise, but they dwindled quickly. However, Bernie quickly noticed another trend. Within a few months of the lamps' release, several larger and better-established lighting firms began replicating Modeline's Sofglo fiberglass shades. Whereas other business owners may have been disturbed by this, Bernie was pleased. The lighting industry was starving for new ideas. Thus, even though Bernie was not experiencing a significant profit, it was apparent that Modeline had struck a chord.

Modeline's 1947 award-winning "Torso." *Copyright Modeline Co.*

Modeline Model 345, 1947. *Photographer Libby Danforth*

Modeline's sophomore offering, in March 1947, was a line of fifteen lamps displaying anthropomorphic forms carved from wood. A couple dancing, a male torso, a woman's profile, and others were in this series of artful lamps. One of them—a woman's torso—caught more than just the attention of buyers. It was selected for display by the New York

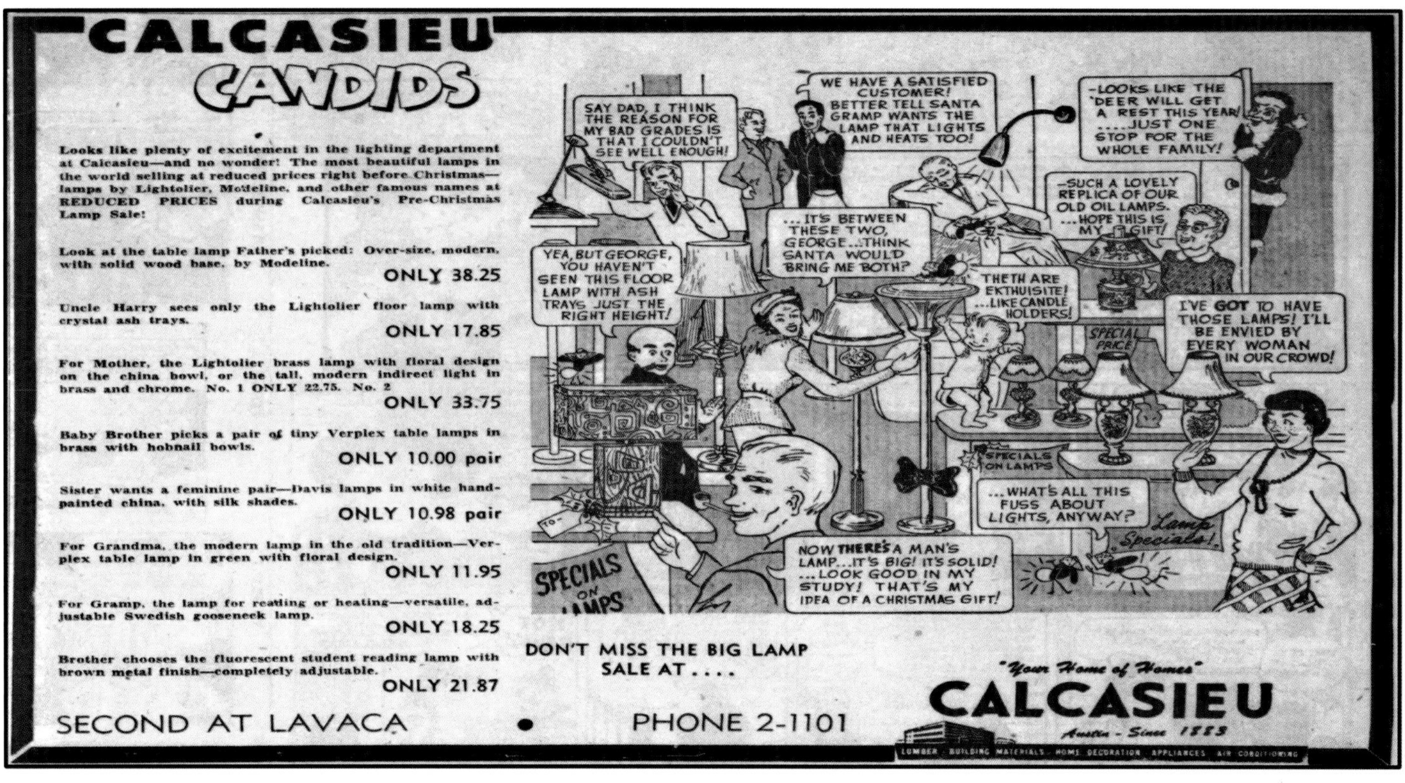

Museum of Modern Art in September 1947. This further confirmation of Modeline's venture into wooden lighting was all that Bernie needed to double down. He ramped up the hiring of factory employees and scaled up production to pursue dealers outside Southern California. This increased production was threatened in February 1948, when the construction of the Harbor Freeway eliminated the rear access and shipping dock at the Diamond Street factory. This forced Modeline to relocate. Fortunately, the 27,000-square-foot warehouse at 120 North Beaudry Avenue (adjacent to the Diamond Street location) had recently been vacated. This warehouse, combined with the attached office at 110 North Beaudry, had all the space that Modeline would need to continue its growth.

Even with the added space and growing staff, Modeline still needed to address the desires of consumers. If the firm was to create something that would hold buyers' attention for more than a few months, it needed to be far more complex, more modern, and more challenging to replicate. Modeline needed to outsource the design. Most lighting companies found it most economical to have an in-house design team, but Bernie opted to use the same structure as Brown-Saltman. He subcontracted designers and paid them a royalty per lamp sold. This structure motivated the designer to always be at work in pursuit of the next great creation. It also saved Modeline much-needed cash on the front end. With what at that point was an unnecessarily large factory and a factory staff of thirteen well-trained individuals, the time had come to test the upper limits of Modeline's capabilities. In line with the idea behind Modeline's inception, and inspired by the success of the anthropomorphic lamps, Bernie did not initially seek out an architect or furniture designer. Instead, he approached the renowned sculptor Lynn Lawrence. Lynn was a skilled artist who had already designed several plaster lamps. Bernie shared his vision with her for the future of Modeline's lamp production and asked her to design a lamp of seemingly impossible form. Something elegant but not ostentatious. There seemed to be little purpose in having a factory outfitted with custom and complex machinery if they were unable to produce a lamp that would require such sophisticated tooling. Bernie wanted to give buyers a lamp that could have come only from Modeline and to introduce them to a new type of lighting. In October 1948, Lynn made this possible. She presented a line of eleven unique table, floor, and desk lamps of sculpted ash to Bernie and Esther. Not only did she exceed Bernie's expectations for the bases, but Lynn took the molded Sofglo fiberglass to a more complex level by integrating it seamlessly into the design. These sculptures were inarguably stately and wholly modern. They extricated any tribute to their atomic ancestors and ran headlong into what Bernie believed was the lamp of the future. Perhaps most importantly, as Modeline introduced itself to American consumers, the bases were composed entirely of wood. No more metal support structure or bent-wire accents. Before this point, ceramic, plaster, and iron dominated the American lighting industry. Modeline's new sculpted lamps would surely catch the eyes of all who beheld them, and make for easy coordination with furniture. The first advertisements for these lamps went as far as to display them perched atop a tree trunk to emphasize their natural, earthy beauty.

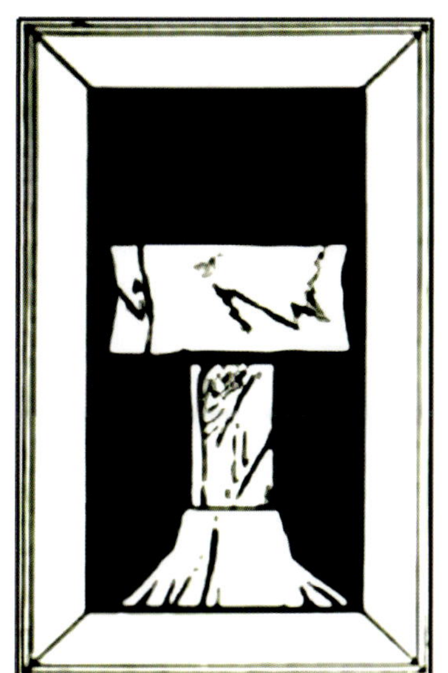

Copyright Modeline Co.

Immediately upon their release, Lynn Lawrence's designs launched Modeline into a new era. Modeline lamps became one of the most popular home furnishings of 1948 and 1949. They were offered in seven finishes of walnut, cordovan, antique white, natural, teak, ebony, and fruitwood. Coordinating interior lighting with furniture had never been easier. The sudden demand for these lamps sparked a wave of attention from dealers, designers, and design critics across the country. Their presence in furniture dealers and showrooms grew from a handful of shops in Southern and central California to being a mainstay in twelve states.

Feeling that a little bit of security had been won for his firm, Bernie began injecting his ideals into Modeline. He opted against seeking additional factory staff through the conventional means of newspaper classifieds. Instead, he began what he called "second-chance hiring." Inmates at the Chino Prison, many of whom had become skilled woodworkers while incarcerated, were hired through the parole board as part of their societal rehabilitation. "Most parolees turn out to be good workers," Bernie said in an interview in the *Daily News Post*. "If they get in trouble, they do it someplace else, not on the job. A parolee who is earning a living does not have to depend on a welfare check to support his family. Then, too, there's a great deal of personal satisfaction in seeing an ex-offender do a good job and straighten himself out." This sentiment became inherent to Modeline. Bernie demonstrated that open-mindedness and progressive values could be espoused successfully without sacrificing the profitability.

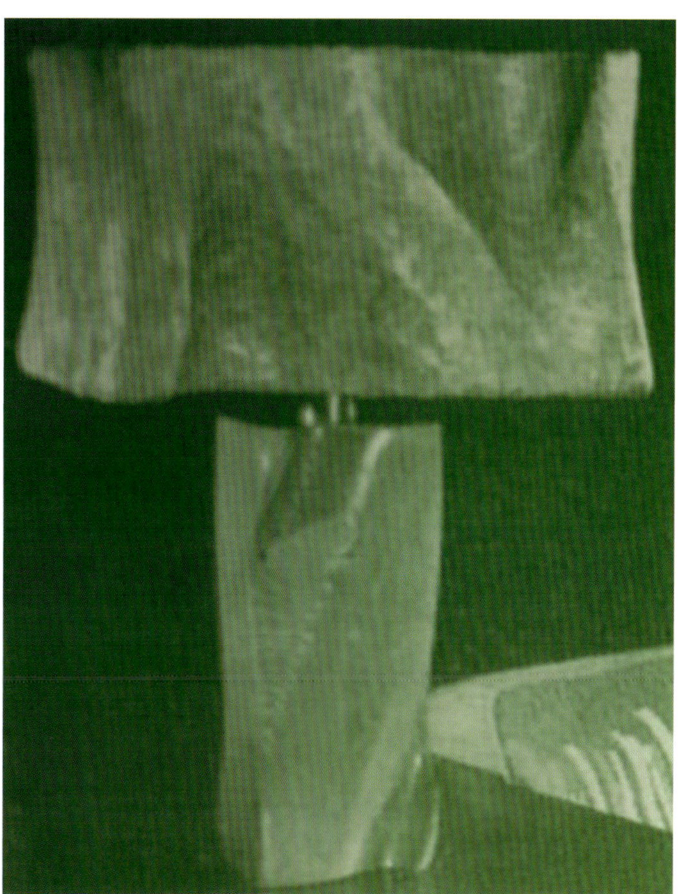

Lynn Lawrence's 1948 sculpted ash table lamp and Sofglo shade. *Copyright Modeline Co.*

With additional hiring of executive and managerial staff, the factory required less of the Robertses' direct attention. Bernie and Esther began appearing at furniture trade shows around the country. Bernie found that he was born for this environment. He was quick witted, gregarious, and universally liked. Esther was

From left to right: Shirley Roberts, George Roberts (Bernie's brother), Esther Roberts, Bernie Roberts, Roselle Naftal, and Carl Naftal. *Courtesy of Randi Måvestrand*

introverted, but her genuine nature and kind spirit made her equally beloved. While these events were curated to generate new accounts, they were also treated as weekend getaways for many attendees. Inevitably, the likability of the executive, salesman, or buyer determined the fruitfulness of the trade show. Bernie and Esther were extremely likable, and they were quickly adopted into these professional families. Each event led to more invitations and, before long, the Robertses' weekends were consumed by socializing with the who's who of the furniture industry. This perpetual networking, combined with the success of the Lynn Lawrence lamps, introduced Modeline of California into the lexicon of furniture executives and interior designers throughout the country.

CHAPTER 3

Modeline of California and Its Discontents

As 1950 ended, Bernie Roberts began to hone a more exact business model for Modeline. With the small factory staff and quickly growing profits, Bernie was able to pay the factory workers a considerably higher rate than other lamp and furniture manufacturers were offering. The designers also enjoyed a large 10 percent royalty, which was virtually unheard of. In the November 1950 union contract negotiations, Bernie explained that he intended to double the factory staff by the end of 1951 and that new hires would be paid 30 percent less than current factory employees. This would not affect the wages of current employees, but the staff worried that this would incentivize their dismissal and replacement. Bernie assured them that he had no desire to repeat the four-year headache that was training cabinetmakers to construct wooden lamps, and that nobody's job was in jeopardy. This logic was accepted by most in Gus Brown's Independent Furniture Workers Union, but there was one very vocal dissenter—Gus Parra. Gus had been with Modeline since 1947, and he had, up to this point, maintained a good relationship with Bernie. The proposition of a future factory staff that was paid a reduced rate did not sit well with Gus, and he refused to accept it. Bernie met with him and explained that even with a 30 percent reduction, the Modeline factory staff was making 20 percent more than the average furniture worker in Los Angeles. This reduction was a necessary part of expanding the production at Modeline, and any other prospect could threaten the brand's future. Fearing that he might be in the wrong or making an unethical decision, Bernie met with his lawyer, William B. Esterman. Esterman was very experienced with unions, having represented them in the past. He advised Bernie that he was justified in his concerns about maintaining such an inflated rate for all future hires, and that he was within his rights to propose the future reduction. So Bernie maintained his position. Gus Parra refused future discussions with Bernie and began encouraging the rest of the staff to do the same. So when Gus began riding the time clock, perhaps to send a message to his superiors, Bernie felt that the best course of action would be to let him go. Manuel Diego, head of the shop committee, took issue with the firing of Gus Parra, saying that Bernie could not fire an employee without following the procedures in the union contract. Diego contacted the business agent Gus Brown, who came to the Modeline factory and suggested that the question

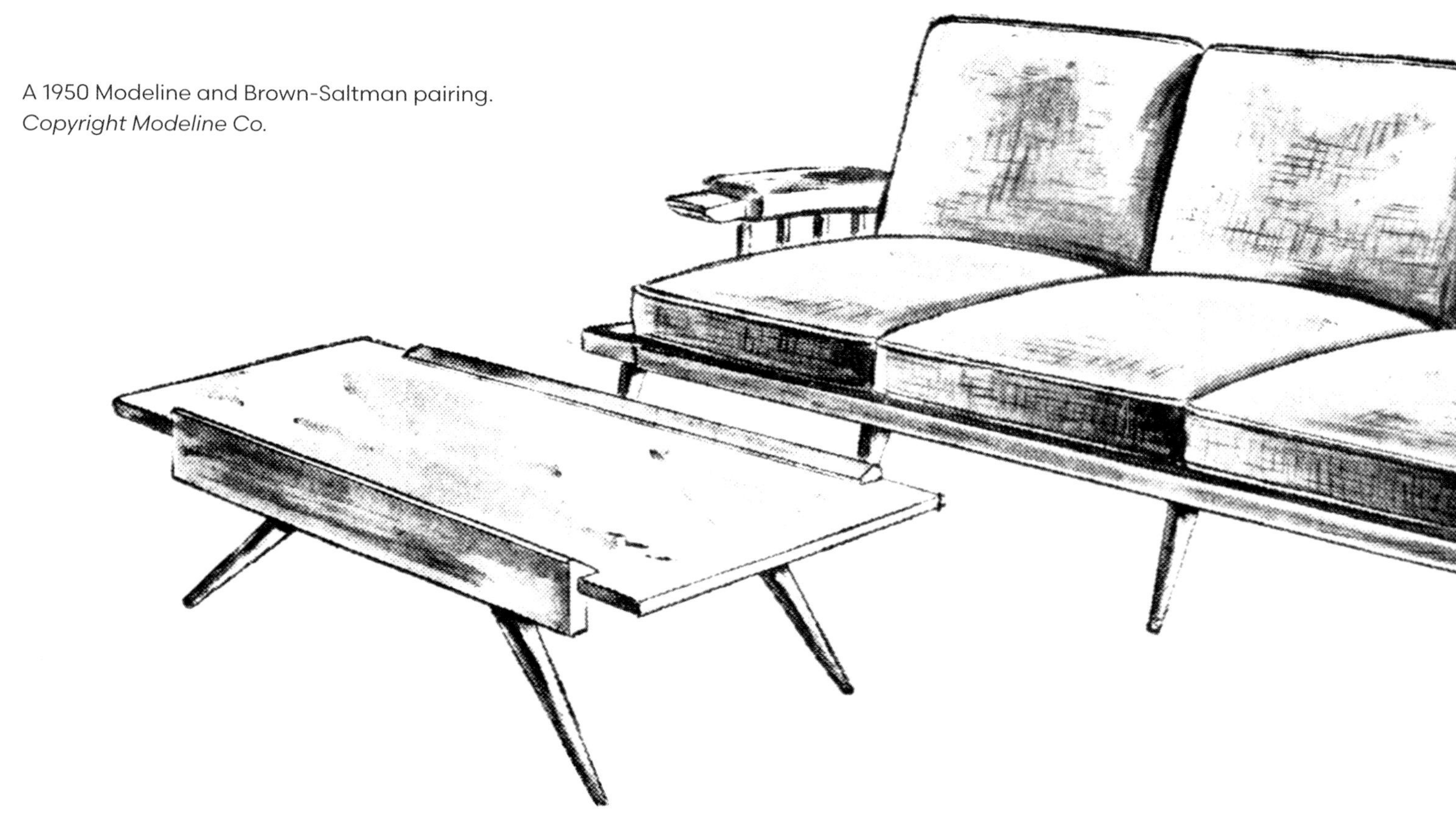

A 1950 Modeline and Brown-Saltman pairing.
Copyright Modeline Co.

of Gus Parra's firing be taken to arbitration. Bernie said that this was absurd, and that Parra was clearly being an insubordinate and dishonest employee. Gus Brown and Bernie Roberts reached this point of contention with no clear path forward, and in December 1950 the factory went on strike.

This strike crippled Modeline's ability to fulfill orders and made it nearly pointless to design anything new. While all hell broke loose at the factory, the seeds that Bernie had sown in the furniture industry began to sprout. In a clear picture of the dueling worlds in which Bernie was entrenched, he was elected president of the California Lamp and Shade Manufacturers Association as well as named a board member of California Home Furnishings. His celebration of these achievements, which took place during a furniture show at the Biltmore Hotel in Los Angeles, was interrupted when a group of over a hundred picketers as well as members of the Los Angeles Independent Progressive Party showed up to hand out leaflets informing buyers of the current strike and urging them not to buy Modeline lamps.

The strike continued into 1951. Tensions began to boil over when shop foreman Ray Reinhart, unable to pass through the line of picketers to enter the factory, brandished a pistol to part the crowd. This was greeted by union outrage and a demand that punitive actions be taken against Reinhart. However, after law enforcement considered the details of the situation, no legal actions were taken against Reinhart. Assistant city attorney H. D. Taylor, however, did instruct Reinhart to stop carrying a firearm to work. Suffice it to say that union members were not pleased. This lack of action on the part of Taylor poured gasoline on the fire. In a response to the apparent lack of consideration for picketers' safety, Reinhart was jumped and badly beaten by two picketers one morning while he was attempting to open the factory. For his injuries, he spent three days in the hospital, and the Modeline factory, for the first time since the beginning of the strike, fully ceased operations. While the factory was closed, strikers put a water hose through the mail slot and flooded the building, resulting in thousands of dollars' worth of damage to equipment and materials. The strikers, feeling a moment of victory over their employer, turned the strike into a block party. By the sixteenth week of the strike, live music, dancing, and street food were regular occurrences at the picket line. The Youth Committee for the Modeline Strikers even wrote and performed a one-act play, which was a dramatized narration of the firing of Gus Parra.

Bernie desperately sought an end to all the madness, and renegotiation began. After a bitter exchange of opinions and the release of months of pent-up frustration, Bernie drew a line at a reduction of new-hire wage of 10 percent. Still refusing to accept, the Gus Brown Furniture Workers Union filed charges of unfair labor practices with the National Labor Relations Board. This petition was swiftly dismissed, but the strike still did not end until May 1951. Ultimately, Bernie agreed not to change the wages of new hires. He could not, however, overcome the feeling that he had been betrayed by the same union that he had fought many times to defend. Worse yet, he had become a public enemy in the eyes of several union publications in the Los Angeles area. One of these magazines—*People's World*—Bernie had even personally bankrolled when it fell on hard financial times in 1950. This fact did not keep them from characterizing him as a greedy boss when the strike erupted.

Bernie officially renounced his membership to the Communist Party in 1951 and registered as a Democrat. Beyond all the drama, Modeline had suffered a potentially fatal wound. Bernie again sought the advice and assistance of Percy Solotoy.

A mid 1950s lighted table designed by John Keal.
Photographer Michelle Seal

CHAPTER 4

The Dream Team

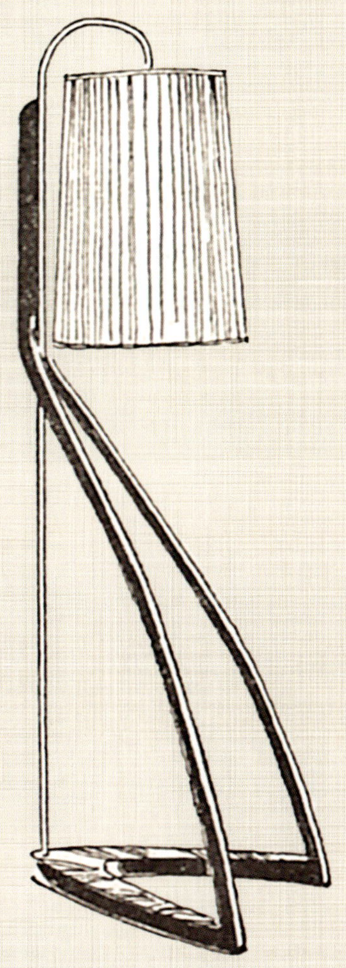

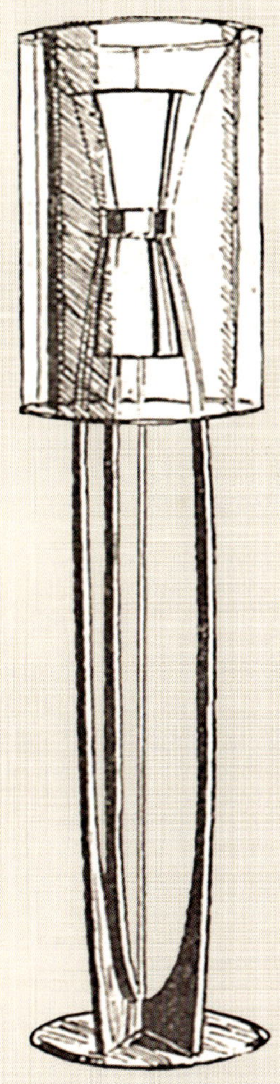

Arthur Jacobs. *Courtesy of Jeff Jacobs*

The promising financial outlook of the Lynn Lawrence era at Modeline had been slowed to a near halt by the strike and the subsequent inability to fulfill orders quickly. As the demand for these designs also began to slow, Bernie feared that Modeline could soon be added to the long list of failed enterprises of postwar America. Modeline's good fortune, however, would soon be preserved by a twenty-nine-year-old retired Air Corps pilot who was, at this moment, working as a display maker in San Francisco for Macy's department store.

Arthur Jacobs had obtained a bachelor's degree in mathematics from Beloit College before relocating to San Francisco with his wife, Peggy, to study industrial design. Arthur had submitted many of his furniture and lighting designs to design competitions in the late 1940s, in hopes that one of them may lead to more artistically fulfilling employment. One such competition, the West Coast Decorative Arts Competition, put on by the San Francisco Museum of Art, saw Arthur Jacobs place in both the lighting and furniture design categories in January 1951. While the lighting-design category had been sponsored by Bulmore Manufacturing Co., the furniture category, in which Arthur placed first, was sponsored by Brown-Saltman. The winning piece was a "convertible dresser" that featured a foldout vanity and a center section in which one could hang neckties and sport coats. It was more of a compact closet than a traditional dresser, and it displayed the genius of its designer for the implementation of clever features created for increased practicality. Also among Jacobs's furniture design submissions was a convertible coffee table that folded up to become a small, upholstered bench.

Arthur Jacobs's 1951 convertible dresser. *Courtesy of Jeff Jacobs*

Courtesy of Jeff Jacobs

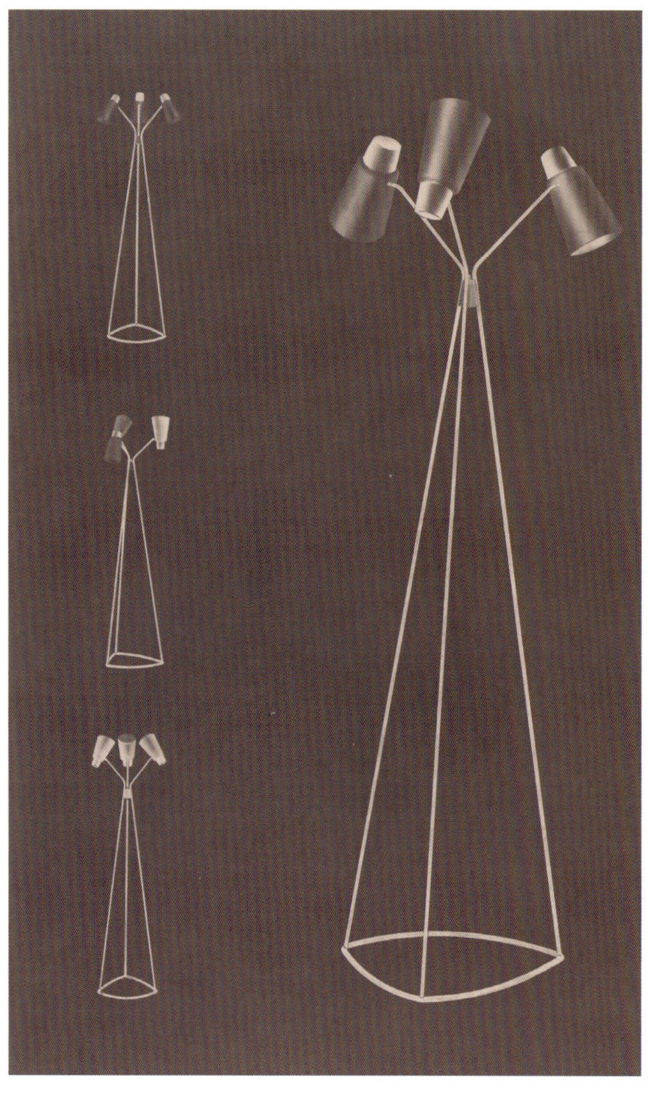

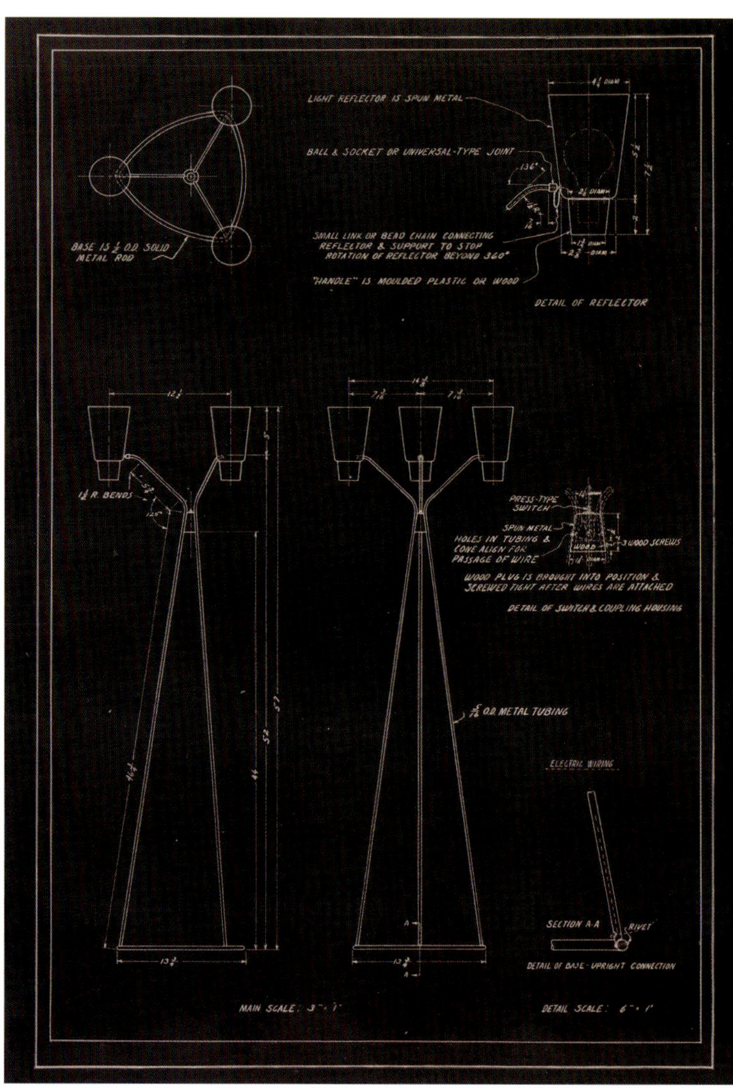

Courtesy of Jeff Jacobs

Arthur Jacobs's lamp design submission to the 1951 West Coast Decorative Arts Competition.
Courtesy of Jeff Jacobs

Even before the establishment of a career in design, a clear set of themes could be seen among these pieces—modern, practical, natural, and always designed with a trick function. These themes made perfect sense in the context of Arthur Jacobs's passions. Outside of a love of and fascination with aviation and the complications therein, Jacobs was an amateur naturalist. The little free time that he had was consumed with hiking, camping, and fly fishing.

Arthur Jacobs was, in all these ways, a perfect match for Modeline of California. So, when Bernie Roberts asked Percy Solotoy in the summer of 1951 what should be done to bring Modeline back onto the correct trajectory, Percy happily supplied Arthur Jacobs's contact information. Bernie was fortunate in that Arthur had already seen and been impressed with the Lynn Lawrence lamps, so the strong sales pitch that Bernie had prepared proved to be largely unnecessary. After a series of phone calls to flesh out ideas and explore future possibilities, Bernie won the confidence of this promising young designer. Jacobs agreed to design a trial run of lamps for Modeline. His level of commitment to the firm would hinge on their success or lack thereof. After a few months of experimentation, Jacobs presented a design that he felt would be consistent with the brand. This first Arthur Jacobs design for Modeline was a table lamp and a floor lamp twin, which consisted of an iron wire tripod supporting two conjoined ash balls. Its shade was of Sofglo fiberglass, and in Jacobs's signature style, it featured the trick function of having the angle of the shade adjustable within presets for both direct and indirect lighting. Its appearance was awkwardly top heavy and almost alien. It was, above all other characteristics, unique from the offerings of other lighting firms.

Arthur Jacobs's convertible coffee table.
Courtesy of Jeff Jacobs

Arthur Jacobs's adjustable-angle tripod lamp. *Courtesy of JF Chen*

Another particularly appealing feature at the time was the relatively low cost of production. If this lamp connected with the market, it could breathe some much-needed life back into the now-struggling brand. Production began quickly, and like Lynn Lawrence's designs before it, this simple little lamp sold incredibly well. The ingenious simplicity of this lamp caught the eye of consumers and designers, and the praises of this novel design were sung universally among them. Among those fascinated with this new model was one particularly influential rising star in the world of modern architecture. University of Southern California student Pierre Koenig chose to use the floor lamp in the staging of his first house "No. 1."

Pierre Koenig's "No. 1"

The overwhelmingly positive response to Arthur Jacobs's first design for Modeline gave Jacobs the confirmation that he had been seeking. In February 1952, Arthur and Peggy Jacobs relocated from San Francisco to Los Angeles for Arthur to work more closely with Modeline. His sophomore design at Modeline was a brilliant table lamp that gave the user even more placement options than did the tripod lamp. Mr. Imp, as Jacobs called it, was a gooseneck lamp with two pliable metal legs protruding from the base. This allowed it to be placed at any desired angle, hooked over a headboard, hung on a wall, or manipulated to fit nearly any other imaginable position. Mr. Imp was quickly a fan favorite in showrooms.

Arthur Jacobs's Mr. Imp. The fiberglass shade design was inspired by the "droop nose" that was becoming popular in supersonic aircraft designs at the time. *Copyright Modeline Co.*

Koenig was not the only academic to take notice of the buzz surrounding Modeline of California. A design professor at both the University of California and Los Angeles Art Center School, John Keal, took an interest in the firm. Keal, who also happened to be a top designer at Brown-Saltman, had been familiar with Modeline since the time of its

John Keal. *Copyright Modeline Co.*

inception. He had his hands full with teaching as well as designing for nine other California furniture manufacturers, and his level of interest in what up to this point had been a new and struggling firm was minimal. Being a man who was abundantly familiar with the difficulty of turning a business in financial freefall into a respected and profitable one, he was impressed both with Bernie's leadership and Arthur's unique design style. He believed that Modeline had only just begun to scratch the surface of its potential success, and that he could contribute something meaningful that would carry the company to its maximum potential.

John Keal's design work was all about individuality and coordination. These were two already strong themes in Modeline's growing body of work. Keal wanted every person who purchased one of his pieces to feel that there was no daylight between their personal tastes and the features of his designs. Because of this dedication to preserving buyer autonomy, John Keal was less bound to the growing trend of minimalism in modern design. Keal would often implement a Victorian, art deco, or colonial detail if it meant offering a piece that would be exactly right for a certain type of buyer. This was slightly out of sync with Modeline's push deeper into European- and Asian-influenced modernism, but Bernie felt that Keal had a proven record of success with this. John Keal also offered a voice of experience regarding staying power in the furniture industry. A brand could not be original alone. Consumers quickly forgot about originality when it conflicted with their preferences. If a new firm was to weather the always-changing tastes of the American consumer, it had to predict trends before they changed. It had to consider its sales to be as valuable for their market data as they were for profitability. Keal officially joined the Modeline team as a designer in the summer of 1952, and by autumn his role grew to be the design director. As design director, his role was to seek out new design talent, curate the designs that he felt would best suit the Modeline brand, and inform the materials buyer on what he felt would be the best woods and shade materials from which to create new models. Being a university lecturer, Keal was also uniquely well positioned to funnel fresh talent into Modeline.

A 1952 John Keal–designed table lamp. *Copyright Modeline Co.*

A 1952 John Keal–designed floor lamp. *Copyright Modeline Co.*

MODERN TOUCH—A wire and ash cone base with a Polylyn plastic shade feature the new table lamp at left by Modeline of California. At right is Modeline's floor lamp of ash, with a central column of brass and a shade of Sof-Glo Fiberglass.

Copyright Modeline Co.

Arthur Jacobs and John Keal joined forces to design for the spring 1953 brochure as Bernie directed his focus to getting the 1951 and 1952 models in front of more buyers. Solving both the issue of a need for greater exposure and the need for an influx of cash, Bernie struck a deal with the San Fernando Valley Building Contractors Association for Modeline lamps to be used in the staging of 1953's Parade of Homes. The Parade of Homes was an ambitious experiment that consisted of the construction and furnishing of twenty-one homes in the Van Nuys neighborhood of Los Angeles. The idea was to display the latest trends in design and architecture to potential buyers and allow them to purchase these homes fully furnished.

As John Keal's participation in the executive functions at Modeline increased, Bernie and Esther became freer to resume spending time away from the office. Perpetually shuffling from hotel to airport, the couple dove back into furniture trade shows and related outings. Often showing up to these shows as an entire extended family, with Shirley, Carl and Roselle Naftal, their daughter Rita, and Bernie's brother George, they quickly gained a reputation as the life of the party. The Robertses were the lively bunch with the exciting new lamp company, and everyone wanted to get to know them. Even other lighting executives viewed Bernie as more of a comrade than a rival. As far as Bernie's relationship with executives in the furniture business, Modeline was truly in its own class. By its focus on coordinating lighting and furniture, Modeline did more to help case goods manufacturers than arouse feelings of envy among them. With the friendships that developed at these trade shows, the line between work and play practically disappeared. Furniture shows, design award ceremonies, and philanthropic and political fundraisers turned into late nights of cocktails, cigarettes, and storytelling. These outings had the Robertses rubbing shoulders with many influential individuals, and that meant a lot in Los Angeles in the 1950s. To be a jetsetter at this moment in history was a thing so glamorous that few possessed the imagination to dream it up. Ballrooms, banquets, and lavish cocktail parties with executives, political figures, movie stars, and musicians became normal occurrences for Bernie and Esther. This was not without effect on Modeline. For better or worse, Modeline employees were locked into a very generous pay rate. With overhead high and popularity on the rise, the shift began in 1953 away from Modeline representing itself as *only* being America's foremost producer of clever wooden lighting. From this point forward, an emphasis was placed in Modeline's catalogs and advertisements on the luxurious and refined quality of Modeline lamps. This was no problem for Arthur Jacobs, whose newest creations were looking just as fit for a modern art museum as they were for a living room.

Opposite: One of John Keal's early 1950s Modeline table lamps. *Photographer Libby Danforth*

One of John Keal's early 1950s Modeline table lamps. *Photographer Libby Danforth*

Arthur Jacobs's 1954 table lamps, debuting the hourglass wooden pull switches. *Photographer Libby Danforth*

Rita Naftal, Bernie Roberts, and Esther Roberts. *Courtesy of Randi Måvestrand*

From left to right: Rita Naftal, Carl Naftal, Roselle Naftal, Bernie Roberts, Esther Roberts. *Courtesy of Randi Måvestrand*

Bernie's brother and Modeline CPA Sidney Roberts (*right*) with his father-in-law Morris Eisenshtat (*left*), 1961. *Copyright Modeline Co.*

Standing, left to right: Sam Moss, William Little, Emil Goldhaber, Bernie Roberts. *Seated, left to right*: Raymond Reed, Max Robb, Vic Christy, Louis Neuwirth, Sol Bersch, Al Green. *Copyright Modeline Co.*

The evolution of what would become Modeline's best-selling model began in 1954 with the introduction of Arthur Jacobs's most clever innovation to date. This invention, which was showcased on a series of five floor and table lamps, changed both the visual presentation of Modeline lamps and the experience of turning them on. The addition of a sculpted-wood detail was present on these lamps. This shapely block, when pulled, would activate the lamp. When pulled again, the brightness was changed from high to medium. And when pulled a third time, the lamp became dim. Never had lamp lighting been such an enjoyable process. Far from it—the activation of a lamp had not previously been taken into consideration by any designer to any meaningful extent. In the design of a utility, there is the first designer and then there is the designer who takes the innovation to its most refined form. In the case of this ingenious switch, Arthur Jacobs assumed both roles. The initial version of this switch, which appeared at furniture showrooms in 1954, was a wide, ash hourglass that attached to the socket via a thin, hidden rod. The second iteration, appearing seven months later, in early 1955, was a tapered, more streamlined version that attached to the socket via a concealed chain.

Meanwhile, in Jacobs's personal life, he was celebrating the birth of his first son. To provide a comfortable life for his growing family, he sought additional employment to augment his royalty income from Modeline. This came in the form of becoming the principal designer at a second new Los Angeles

brand—Prudential Lighting. Prudential created commercial fixtures, and Jacobs quickly became their most valuable asset. While Arthur reserved his more artistic expressions for Modeline, he took great pride in his commercial lighting designs. As these fixtures became common throughout commercial buildings inside and outside California, he was often known to pause upon entering a building, look up at the ceiling, and smile to see his handiwork.

Back at Modeline, marketing continued to target a wealthier clientele, and the designs became sleeker and more sophisticated as a result. Gone were the days of the bulky wooden bases and thick, Sofglo fiberglass shades. There was a challenge faced by the designers, though, and that was to design lamps with dainty wooden structures that appeared to be impossibly thin while also maintaining enough structural integrity not to wobble or warp over time. Arthur Jacobs's solution to this was to implement a hidden support system by relying on the strength of the steel shade rings. The rings, when mounted inside rather than on top of the wooden frame, allowed the lower base joinery to be sufficient in providing structural integrity without any additional wooden reinforcement. This feature was first displayed in Jacobs's 1955 "Tree Lamp," as he called it. The Tree Lamp featured a slimmed-down version of the carved-wood switch. Also new for 1955 was a name for this clever apparatus—the Modeliter. The Tree Lamp also introduced what would become a mainstay in Modeline lamp designs—the "dimensional shade." Jacobs, being an outdoorsman who rarely took a weekend trip without his fly-fishing gear in tow, lifted the inspiration for this idea directly from nature. In the way that the branches of a tree created the silhouette of a larger form than the trunk alone, the Tree Lamp's wooden base appeared to grow directly through the floating, semitransparent outer shade. This feature created superior light diffusion while simultaneously muting the glare that plagued other shade makers. These undeniably unique features received the high praise of everyone from designers to Modeline's competitors. The Tree Lamp was hailed as the most significant advancement in interior lighting design of the twentieth century so far. This acclaim, combined with Bernie's high marks on likability among other firms, landed Bernie in a place at the epicenter of American lamp manufacturers. In May 1955 he was elected president of the Lamp and Shade Institute of America.

Arthur Jacobs's 1955 Tree Lamp.
Photographer Libby Danforth

Arthur Jacobs with his first son. *Courtesy of Jeff Jacobs*

Opposite: Natural-motif, adjustable-angle table lamps by Arthur Jacobs. *Photographer Libby Danforth*

MODERN AS TOMORROW

Every lamp in our collection is available in many colorings, multi-lacquered for smoothness and harmony; with shades to harmonize with the most "difficult" rooms.

With the question of structural integrity answered by Arthur Jacobs's dimensional shade within a shade, only one item remained on John Keal's to-do list for Modeline in 1955. The brand's reputation as the highest-quality and most creative manufacturer of wooden lighting was virtually unchallenged. However, the only wood choices on the Modeline menu were ash and oak. Bernie Roberts and John Keal rightly felt that offering a wide variety of wood options would not be economical, so the tonal variety available to the customer was limited to the finish rather than the wood itself. Oak and ash furniture were becoming antiquated, and the design team feared that the harsh, wide grain of Modeline lamps would become difficult to coordinate with the modern home furnishings of teak and walnut. If a new material was to be selected, it would have to be as lightly colored as possible in its natural, unfinished form to make for ease of applying wood toner. This ruled out the popular choices of the time of walnut and teak. After months of sampling and experimentation, the answer arrived in the form of African limba. Limba, known more commonly at the time as korina, is a wood that is as lightly colored as spruce but a bit harder. It also had the benefit of having some attractive grain that would take on the appearance of some of the more exotic-looking woods when finished strategically. The transition to this new material began in mid-1955, and by early 1956 the factory was exclusively using korina imported from the Congo.

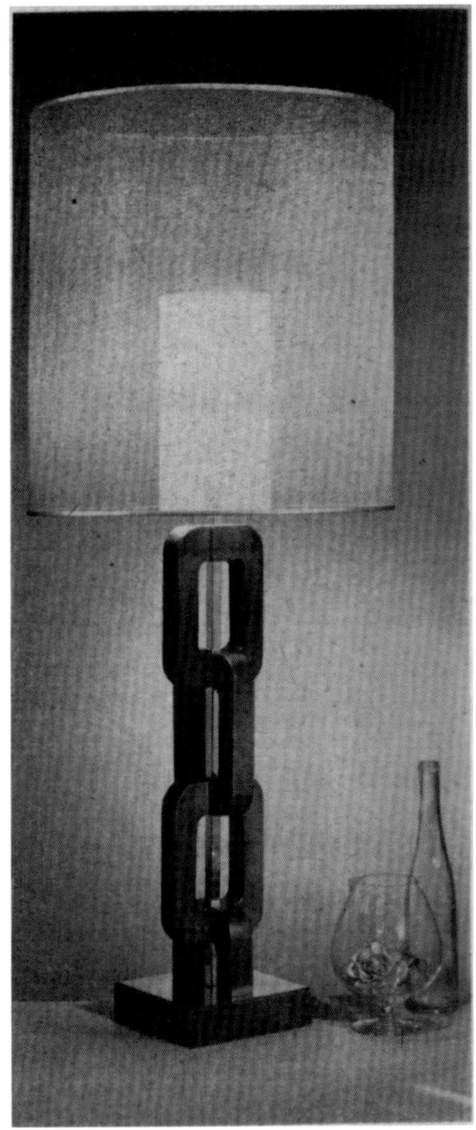

Arthur Jacobs's "Chain" table lamp, ca. 1956. *Copyright Modeline Co.*

Opposite: Photographer Libby Danforth

As Modeline entered its tenth year, the experiment in modern wooden lighting was proving to be an extremely successful one. Sales were strong and trending upward in every market. Modeline had permanent showrooms in Los Angeles, San Francisco, Chicago, and New York, as well as dealers in every state and exports to Hawaii, Canada, and Mexico. To celebrate Modeline's tenth anniversary as well as his fourth year at the firm, Arthur Jacobs presented his third and final evolution of the Modeliter-equipped Tree Lamp, which was shown for the first time in living color in Modeline's 1956 catalog—the Model 350. As Jacobs's first major work in korina, the Model 350 was an exercise in highlighting the merits of this new material. A brass-capped korina base and a trispire korina standard supported a thin fiberglass interior shade. Perched below the interior shade was a Modeliter pull switch that appeared to be suspended in space. All of this was encased in Jacobs's now-characteristic dimensional, light-diffusing outer shade—available both in Open Weave and Lurex material options. The Model 350 was a slimmed-down and streamlined descendant of the Tree Lamp, with all superfluous details removed. What was left after reducing the Tree Lamp to only its most attractive and useful characteristics was a floor lamp and a corresponding table lamp (the Model 1545) that defined modern lighting in its most elegant expression.

Arthur Jacobs's 1956 Model 350.
Photographer Paige Hood

The Model 1545. *Photographer Libby Danforth*

Photographer Libby Danforth

Models 350 and 1545 made their debut to thunderous acclaim at Los Angeles Furniture Mart in February 1956. They were widely hailed by design critics as the most modern and clever American lamps ever produced. For this moment in time, the entire design world was looking at Modeline. Amid the celebration of Modeline's impressive new body of work, Arthur Jacobs dove back into his craft, not even for a second resting on his laurels. Summer had not yet come before he presented fourteen new models to John Keal and Bernie Roberts, each somehow more attractive than the last.

Copyright Modeline Co.

The Martin House, Nashville, Tennessee.
Photographer Libby Danforth

A 1956 Modeliter-equipped floor lamp by Arthur Jacobs. *Photographer Libby Danforth*

Opposite: As Arthur Jacobs begun implementing the dimensional shade on more models, these shades performed a larger role in the overall design than any traditional lampshade before them. *Photographer Libby Danforth*

The year 1956 brought Modeline's most rapid period of growth to date. By the end of the year, the factory staff had grown to forty-eight men and women, while sixteen national salesmen traveled the country and managed dealer relationships. Shirley, who had recently graduated from UCLA, split her time between political activism and office responsibilities, as well as helping stage the permanent showrooms. Modeline's domestic sales were at an all-time high, and its export business was beginning to thrive as it expanded to include Cuba, Venezuela, South Africa, and the Philippines. Bernie and Esther had become celebrities in the furniture industry. There was hardly a showroom grand opening, golf outing, ski trip, trade show, or design panel to which they were not invited. Even at the peak of success, Bernie didn't stray far from the ideals of his younger years, and Shirley was following closely in his footsteps. Donations to and involvement in democratic causes and philanthropic organizations by the Robertses were constant, as well as a sustained belief in the practice of parolee second-chance hiring. It was also common for Bernie, upon the passing away of a colleague in the furniture industry, to rally other executives together to raise money to take care of their respective families. Shirley took great care to ensure that the workers at Modeline were treated with dignity and that nobody was denied a job because of the color of their skin, their religious preference, or their ethnic heritage. When Bernie gave tours of the plant, he was known to stop at each employee to comment on or ask about the goings on in his or her life. This respect and consideration for the personhood of each of these individuals kept Modeline employees feeling appreciated, to the point that it was exceptionally rare for a staff member to quit. The core team of factory workers that had begun careers with Modeline in the late 1940s was still happily employed, and much of the added staff were their friends and families.

With Arthur Jacobs and John Keal becoming increasingly overwhelmed with creating new designs for each catalog, Bernie set out to add talent to the team. Several designers created the lighting equivalent of a single television pilot episode that never saw a full season. Some designers created two or three unique designs but never continued producing for Modeline. One of these new designers, however, would prove to become an indispensable part of Modeline. Jack Haywood was a twenty-eight-year-old army draftsman who was looking to begin a professional career in design and architecture. Bernie had been impressed with

TONY HILL
CERAMICS
(Wholesale & Retail)
3121 West Jefferson Blvd.
Los Angeles, California

L 214 — 43" tall
One of 12 new large lamps in terracotta designed and decorated by Jack Haywood

Opposite: A 1957 Arthur Jacobs–designed floor lamp.
Photographer Libby Danforth

Jack Haywood. *Courtesy of Gar Haywood*

An early 1957 Modeline table lamp designed by Jack Haywood. *Copyright Modeline Co.*

Haywood's terra-cotta lamp designs for Tony Hill Ceramics at the New York Lamp Show in 1955 and followed up with the Los Angeles native shortly thereafter. Haywood was a passionate, highly skilled designer and was excited at the prospect of joining the hottest lighting company in California in the middle of their meteoric rise to national recognition.

Being a Black designer working in a mostly segregated field, Haywood did not want to be limited by anything other than the quality of his work. The only restriction that Modeline designers faced, socially or creatively, was that their designs had to consist primarily of wood. Haywood found this to be an attractive quality in the company. In July 1956, Haywood auditioned a few of his drawings to Keal and Roberts. With the enthusiastic approval of Arthur Jacobs, who was as impressed by Jack's work as John and Bernie had been, Haywood officially joined the Modeline team in October 1956.

Opposite: A 1956 Arthur Jacobs–designed table lamp, equipped with a silent Mercury Switch that glows in the dark. *Photographer Paige Hood*

Photographer Paige Hood

Photographer Paige Hood

Copyright Modeline Co.

With the core design team assembled, Modeline pushed forward into the end of the 1950s, leading the industry in the experiment of creating lamps as thoughtful as the rooms that they lit. Arthur Jacobs, John Keal, and Jack Haywood, under the guidance of Bernie Roberts, ushered in a new age of American lighting. No longer was a lamp an afterthought or a mere utility—it stepped into the foreground. For a hundred years, the lighting industry's focus had been placed mostly and, in many cases, exclusively on the lamp's primary purpose. Upon collective completion of the project of lighting a space without burning it to the ground, Modeline entered the field with this ostensibly obvious idea: that a lamp—like a sofa, wardrobe, or home itself—is an extension of its owner's personality, working in harmony with one's furniture and decor preferences.

The rapid spread of the Modeline style in this era, if it could be reduced to a single cause, had much to do with an idea that originated with Arthur Jacobs. While it is not uncommon to meet a peaceful person, a man of business who takes an active interest in comradery is rare. Jacobs lived by the idea that one's contribution, not their competition, is the defining mark of their success in business. So it flowed as a natural consequence of this belief that Jacobs's concern was placed not on whether he could outperform other designers, but on whether he was contributing in a meaningful way to his field. This allowed the energy that would otherwise have been exhausted in a fearful disposition—worrying about who would create the next big innovation—to be spent in the mastery of his craft. Bernie and Esther lived by similar principles and adopted this same idea. So when the opportunity came to have a clear shot at the competition, the hand of friendship was extended instead. The result of this practice was unsurprising. Rivalry required the active participation of both parties, so Modeline did not need other firms to agree to a ceasefire. They could simply exist in this space—operating under the principles of friendship—without the distraction of an arms race.

An early 1960s lamp table by Arthur Jacobs.
Photographer Libby Danforth

CHAPTER 5

How the West Was Won

Leave It to Beaver. Courtesy of Universal

Below: *The George Burns and Gracie Allen Show.* Courtesy of Sony

The interest in Modeline lamps and the general brand awareness that came about from Pierre Koenig's endorsement and the Parade of Homes was ultimately just as valuable to Bernie Roberts in providing data as in generating sales. A hundred lamps given away but placed strategically in front of the right kind of buyer proved to be far better money spent than the equivalent finances dedicated to traditional advertising. Bernie thought that perhaps the best way to bring in new buyers would not be to spend tens of thousands of dollars in newspaper and magazine ads. Rather, he devised a plan to place Modeline lamps in front of millions of people, and he wouldn't have to spend a dime to do it.

With the celebration of ten years in business and the largest product line rollout to date in 1956, Bernie set out to implement a more targeted version of the free advertising that came from the influence of Pierre Koenig. Television commercials were becoming the most dominant force in advertising, overtaking all other media with ease. So rather than spend an impractical amount of money on commercials, he called everyone that he knew who worked in television—some from recent cocktail parties and some from the days of the Hollywood Black Friday strike—and made appointments to meet with them. He sold set decorators on the merits of Modeline lamps and talked with them about the new designs' growing popularity. He then offered to donate their choice of lamps to be used at their discretion. This proved to be Bernie's most successful marketing tactic to date. The new Arthur Jacobs, John Keal, and Jack Haywood models quickly became the darling of Hollywood, spreading rapidly through film and television sets.

One of the best things about a new idea is that it often captures the attention of the "right people"–for promotion, that is. . . . As a consequence, 10,000,000 viewers recently got an introduction to the new look in lamps when they flicked the switch to the Burns and Allen show, and another 7,000,000 or so were watching them on Jackie Cooper's show. In addition to that wholesale publicity, the lamps have created a considerable stir when they were featured in hotels and motels in the country and when they were used by decorators in furnishing a number of model homes from California to Miami.

—Bernie Roberts, 1957

The Munsters. Courtesy of Universal

A promotional photo of the cast of *Leave It to Beaver*. Courtesy of Getty Images

Natalie Wood with her Arthur Jacobs–designed free-form lamps, 1957. *Courtesy of Getty Images*

Lee Meriwether posing for a Modeline advertisement.
Copyright Modeline Co.

Not only did this new marketing strategy have a strong element of contagion among other set decorators, but it also had the unforeseen effect of capturing the hearts of Hollywood's who's who. As Modeline lamps became prominently featured in television and film sets, they caught the eyes not only of viewers, but of celebrities as well. The tastemakers of Hollywood became Modeline's greatest unpaid spokespeople as their enthusiasm about the exclusivity and luxury of the brand created an unprecedented wave of demand. This uniquely California-style influencer marketing would become a clear precursor for future California brands. Modeline did not have to successfully win over all people to experience monumental success. They simply had to win over the right people. Through creativity, outside-the-box thinking, and a little bit of good luck, Bernie Roberts became a pioneer of this new kind of marketing that would later dominate the world through social media and become the go-to tactic for any serious brand. Through the conscious employment of this strategy, Modeline's marketing was so successful that not only did it win the hearts and business of tens of thousands of buyers throughout the country, but Modeline won the right to define its field. The Modeline style became synonymous with modern lighting. By the end of 1956, the small lamp manufacturer for which bankruptcy had been a near certainty on more than one occasion had confidently secured their place in the American homes of the 1950s.

CHAPTER 6

Inside the Factory

A mid-1960s Arthur Jacobs–designed prototype chain lamp. *Photographer Paige Hood*

The Beaudry Avenue plant had come a long way since 1946, and the sales of the mid-1950s guaranteed greater expansion. What only ten years prior had been a series of makeshift tools operated by a few freshman workers was now a well-oiled machine churning out the finest wooden lamps ever created. By 1957, Modeline's factory had grown to fifty-eight experienced individuals. The korina usage at the plant had grown from 38,000 board feet in 1955 to a staggering 80,000 board feet by the end of 1956. The growth in orders and accounts receivable suggested that that number would double again by the end of 1957. Bernie encouraged the designers to create as many unique models as they could, to strike the iron while it was hot, but the iron did not seem to be cooling. The top three designers were becoming celebrities in the world of design. The unsung heroes at the firm, however, weren't for a

Opposite: A mid-1950s Arthur Jacobs–designed prototype lamp table. *Photographer Libby Danforth*

second forgotten by Bernie, Esther, and Shirley. Many of the factory employees grew up at Modeline, and Bernie viewed and treated them as family.

There was a process through which a Modeline lamp journeyed from the mind of its designer into the home of its owner. Arthur Jacobs, John Keal, and Jack Haywood each had scaled-down woodshops in their homes. One of them would sketch a new design, then create a rough prototype to test the general feasibility of any experimental features. With the completion of the rough prototype and any necessary adjustments, this product was taken to the Modeline plant, where a factory employee would turn out a more refined prototype. This factory-made prototype was then presented to John Keal or Bernie Roberts for review. Some of these models went on to production, and some of them did not. But all of them passed through this process.

A Modeline factory worker in 1959 uses cut tire inner tubes to clamp the base joint of a floor lamp. The use of inner tubes as clamps was common at Modeline, since it provided enough strength to hold the joint but lacked the rigidity that would otherwise damage the wood. The primary bonding agent used in the factory was a cold-setting Willhold glue. After the experimentation of the late 1940s, this was found to be ideal, since the close tolerances did not allow for sufficient heat to reach the inside of the joint to cure a hot-setting glue. *Copyright Modeline Co.*

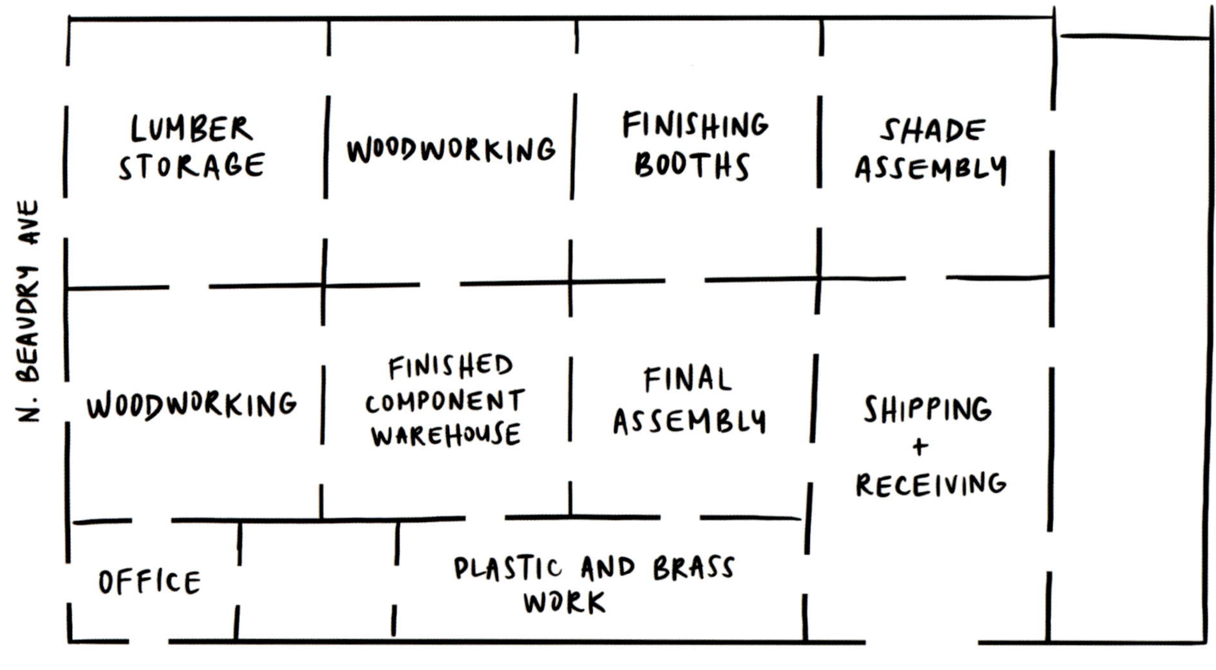

Rendering by Laura Hernandez

Above: A twelve-spindle carving machine allowed one person to perform the work of ten for certain lamp bases. This machine was used on bases that did not have intricate joinery or the need for specialty jigs. *Copyright Modeline Co.*

Right: A factory worker applies a lacquer finish to a row of Model 1525 floor lamps. The lamp bases were secured to a rotating platform, which allowed for an even application of the finish. Although there were many finish options offered at Modeline, the walnut finish accounted for about 90 percent of all lamps sold. In addition to these custom-made finishing stands, the factory used a great number of specialty tools. Employed in various stages of lamp construction were two Delta drill presses, two Buffalo drill presses, a Franklin ripsaw, an Oliver ripsaw, two Towsley Cincinnati bandsaws, an Oliver No. 129 planer, a Consolidated horizontal boring machine, an Oliver lathe, two Porter No. 612 shapers, a Moak joiner, two custom-built sanders, two Ekstrom Carlson and Rodgers belt sanders, a custom-built brush sander, the aforementioned twelve-spindle carving machine by Parten Minnesota, and two custom spray booths outfitted with pneumatic accessories by Binks and DeVilbiss. *Copyright Modeline Co.*

The final assembly area, situated toward the back of the Modeline plant near the shipping dock, is where completed lamp components were assembled into finished products and packaged for transport to showrooms and retail stores. *Copyright Modeline Co.*

The Garrison House, Birmingham, Alabama. *Photographer Liesa Cole*

CHAPTER 7

The Golden Age

LETTERMAN

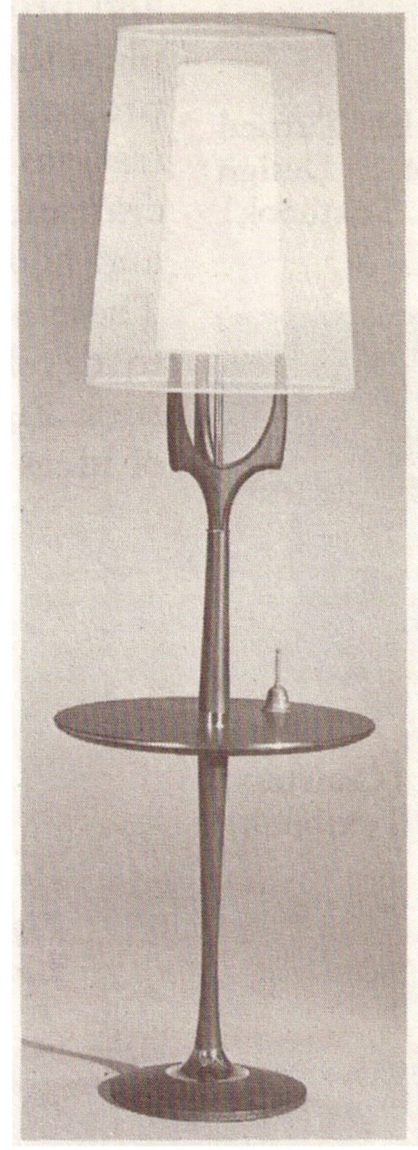

An early 1960s side-table floor lamp by Arthur Jacobs. *Copyright Modeline Co.*

As Modeline began its eleventh year, it did so with the level of respect of a much-older firm. Bernie's primary goal with Modeline—to alter America's view on the role of interior lighting—was achieved far more successfully than he could have dreamed. Buyers at shops across the country were purchasing lamps specifically to coordinate with their furniture, and other lamp manufacturers were taking notice. In the height of the American lighting boom, there began the slow extinction of lamp manufacturers who refused to follow this trend that Modeline had created. Many of the lighting firms that did fall in line did so with a noticeable lack of originality. Majestic Lamp Company, Luxcraft Incorporated, and Guggenheim Company all began offering sculptural, European-influenced wooden lighting in walnut finishes as a direct response to Modeline's success. A few other firms followed Modeline's lead a bit too closely. Sundial Lighting, Lighthouse Lamp and Shade Company, V. H. Woolums, R&J Manufacturing, Roller of California, and Bruce Industries introduced full lines of wooden lamps by the end of 1957 that would have fairly been characterized as Modeline knockoffs. Each consisted of sculptural wood forms, dimensional shades, multiple brightness settings, brass hardware, and, in some cases, even Modeliter switches. Modeline made no effort to bring this imitation to an end. Bernie viewed it all as a clear sign that Modeline was succeeding in changing the expectations and preferences of buyers. Arthur Jacobs agreed with this thinking, so much so that he never sought a design patent for any of his switch innovations or dimensional shades. Nor did he ever express any desire to stop other firms from replicating them.

Jack Haywood established himself as an essential part of Modeline in just his first two years. His work consistently pushed boundaries and played with the question "What does it mean for a lamp design to be modern?" Haywood's experimentation with materials was so extensive that in his home workshop, he was known to incorporate everything from discarded plastic to breakfast cereals in the process of creating his next design. For every hundred designs tried, three or four made it into production at Modeline. This would have been inefficient if not for the fact that Haywood was a relentless workaholic who had given himself entirely to his craft.

Arthur Jacobs's work was not something outside himself. It was the overflow from a deep engagement in the experience of being alive in the world. His inspiration flowed naturally from the two worlds that occupied every corner of his mind—the creation of man and the creation of God and the relationship between those worlds. The biomorphic appearance of Jacobs's lamps was born out of the visions that filled his weekends and afternoons in the foothills of the San Gabriel Mountains.

Opposite: An early 1960s table lamp pair designed by Jack Haywood. *Photographer Libby Danforth*

Photographer Libby Danforth

LIGHTING FOR A LIFETIME

The Modeline collection represents contemporary design and painstaking craftsmanship at their finest. Designed to give the ultimate in effective lighting, each lamp is styled to fit the home of today and to give years of pleasure and service to its owner. Available in a wide variety of colors and finishes, there is a Modeline lamp for your particular lighting problem. For discriminating people who appreciate the finest, it's lamps by Modeline of California.

Arthur Jacobs's Model 1695 table lamp, equipped with a bell-shaped Modeliter switch.
Photographer Libby Danforth

Arthur Jacobs's Model 1930 table lamp, equipped with an egg-shaped Modeliter. *Copyright Modeline Co.*

Arthur, Peggy, Jay, and Jeffrey Jacobs, 1956. *Courtesy of Jeff Jacobs*

Whether camping with his family or fly-fishing alone, Arthur could hardly leave his home without bringing back an idea. His love of the natural world took him so far as to cut large windows into the wall of his basement drafting room, so that even during work, there was never more than a pane of glass between himself and the world that brought him so much joy. His afternoons were spent at his desk sketching out ideas, pausing often to look out at the fruit trees in his backyard where his sons played. These visions of inspiration, when filtered through the mind of a pilot, always came out with some degree of man-made complexity. The Modeliter, Mr. Imp, the adjustable-angle tripod lamp, an adjustable-height floor lamp, and an endless string of designs like them were the byproducts of a man obsessed with technological advancements and their relationship with the natural world.

A late 1950s Arthur Jacobs–designed table lamp. *Copyright Modeline Co.*

Copyright Modeline Co.

John Keal's work at Modeline was a mastery in the craft of coordination and the expression of individuality. Whereas Haywood and Jacobs created lamps that corresponded stylistically to the modern furnishings that were most popular at the time, Keal's involvement in so many other firms allowed him to take this practice to another level entirely. He would often create a detail for a lamp—a unique joint, a colorful enamel inlay, or a piece of carved-wood filigree—which he would then implement in various furniture pieces for other California firms. Keal was unique from Jacobs and Haywood in that he did not commit solely to modern lighting design. Although the term "modern lighting" had been circulating for many years, it was only then, in the late 1950s, beginning to mean anything at all. Up until this point, "modern" was used mostly to describe what a lamp wasn't: traditional. Consequently, a Spanish-, art deco-, or Victorian-style lamp could not rightly have been described as "modern." This didn't bother Keal, since he felt no obligation to be bound by anything more than the tastes of buyers.

A large part of what made the work of these three men so extraordinary is the best-kept secret of design, and that's that it can hardly be taught or transferred. Craftsmanship can be taught, as can the fundamentals and history of design. A designer can also develop and improve their skill over time. One who is not a designer can also learn what makes one design better than another. But the ability to see something beautiful that does not yet exist? That is inborn.

As Modeline's influence increased and other brands adopted the Modeline style, the term "modern lighting" developed a definition. A modern lamp was, in most cases, a minimalist wood-and-brass lamp with a design rooted in naturalism. It is difficult to say whether Keal's use of traditional elements in his designs was a bug or a feature, but it certainly set his designs apart from the other designers, and this was quite important to him. Above all else, John Keal provided Modeline with an eye that had no equal in American furniture manufacturing. His ability to see a design and, in a matter of minutes, determine whether it was fit for production was almost supernatural.

Three table lamps, *from left to right*: Arthur Jacobs, Jack Haywood, Arthur Jacobs. *Photographer Libby Danforth*

The Garrison House, Birmingham, Alabama. *Photographer Liesa Cole*

A 1961 Modeline advertisement displaying two John Keal designs. *Copyright Modeline Co.*

A Modeline advertisement displaying a Martin Aakervik design. *Copyright Modeline Co.*

With new models being put into production multiple times weekly, 1957–1961 saw the largest increase both in terms of individual lamps sold and new models offered. Sales in 1958 were roughly double that of the previous year, and sales in 1959 doubled again. This trend was not a mere side effect of a strong economy, since many other well-established lighting firms were experiencing a decline or stagnation of sales amid the Modeline boom. Modeline's rapid-fire creation of the latest and greatest in lighting seduced even the most disinterested of buyers. A 6-foot-tall trispire floor lamp by Martin Aakervik, a series of jeweled enamel art lamps and a strikingly handsome occasional table floor lamp by John Keal, and a creative hourglass floor lamp by Arthur Jacobs were among the newest offerings. Jack Haywood continued a strong start with a series of lighted room dividers that made for easy transformation of spaces. In addition to these new lamps offered in a variety of wood finishes, Modeline began offering opaque-finish options on certain models of Celadon Green, Mist Blue, and Cafe Au Lait.

But a Rolex? For fifty times the cost there is hardly a gilded screw, and consumers pay for it and display it proudly. The minimalism is not an effect that results from conservative use of materials; it is the point of the design. Any skilled woodworker can churn out products that employ complications far beyond the capabilities of a novice. A genius of design, however, does not have to. Arthur Jacobs could draw a line with a gentle S curvature, place alongside it a straight line, and arrange the shade inside it in just the perfect place. Without adding a superfluous detail, he impressed all who beheld it. Jack Haywood could secure two or three large rectangles by hinges in succession and, without a single element that could have been rightly described as "new," be praised for his originality. Keal could simply eliminate the need for a center standard protruding through the occasional table floor lamp, and it became the envy of all who saw it displayed in a home.

Bernie and Esther at the Los Angeles Furniture Mart Modeline showroom. *Copyright Modeline Co.*

Shirley Roberts demonstrates an extension coffee table by Brown-Saltman at Los Angeles Furniture Mart. *Copyright Modeline Co.*

The sales trends of the late 1950s and early 1960s confirmed that modernism was more than a fad—it was a new way of thinking about design. The European and Asian influence in Modeline's designs advertised a certain cosmopolitan element in the homeowner. The minimalism of delicately sculpted wooden lighting tapped into the thinking that luxury brands use to this day. A cheap wristwatch may tempt the eye with every adornment of gold tones, and it may impress with spinning gears in an open-heart display.

In this period, Modeline opted out of deciding whether to offer quality or quantity. The firm employed enough designers to keep the creative new offerings flowing constantly. Whereas other particularly busy, high-end lighting firms might have used four or five designers over the course of a decade or two, Modeline had already employed Lynn Lawrence, Arthur Jacobs, John Keal, Jack Haywood, John Caldwell, Bill Dorff, Herbert Kornfield, Byron Botker, Martin Aakervik, Robert Levine, and Martin Borenstein by the early 1960s.

Opposite: A mid-1960s John Keal design in ceramic and korina. *Photographer Libby Danforth*

John Keal's 1960 occasional table floor lamp. *Photographer Libby Danforth*

Opposite: A Jack Haywood-designed room divider. *Photographer Paige Hood*

To fully appreciate the effect a Modeline lamp can create—pull the switch, listen to the positive click of a lifetime guaranteed socket, and bathe the immediate area in a glare-free pool of light.

Photographer Libby Danforth

Arthur Jacobs's 1959 "Birdcage" table lamp. *Photographer Paige Hood*

An early 1960s lamp table by Arthur Jacobs. *Photographer Libby Danforth*

The Model 1195 floor lamp by John Keal. *Photographer Libby Danforth*

Six years of strong sales of the Modeliter-equipped models told Bernie that buyers loved easy lamp switches. Before the Modeliter, activating a lamp while seated was a virtual impossibility. Even while standing, large shades made a certain amount of contortion necessary to turn the switch. New for 1961 was Arthur Jacobs's answer to the unrelenting demand for these lazy lamp lighters. Initially conceptualized by Jacobs in 1950, this new base switch required the least possible thought or effort to activate of any lamp switch by any lamp manufacturer in history. Like something out of science fiction, the switch required only a simple tap of the base for the lamp to be illuminated. It did this with the use of a spring-mounted acrylic disk with a design reminiscent of the planetary rings of distant celestial bodies. For this reason, and in keeping with Jacobs's tradition of nomenclature as clever as the switches themselves, it was called the Saturn Switch. The Saturn Switch–equipped Model 8550 table lamp was released to strong acclaim in trial markets of Chicago and New York City, then offered more widely in the spring of 1961. Much to Bernie's chagrin, the Saturn Switch was the successor to the Modeliter solely in terms of innovation. Not only did it fail to overtake the sales of the Modeliter-equipped models, but its sales were so poor as to justify an abrupt and early retirement by the spring of 1962.

Arthur Jacobs's 1961 Model 8550 table lamp, equipped with the Saturn Switch. *Copyright Modeline Co.*

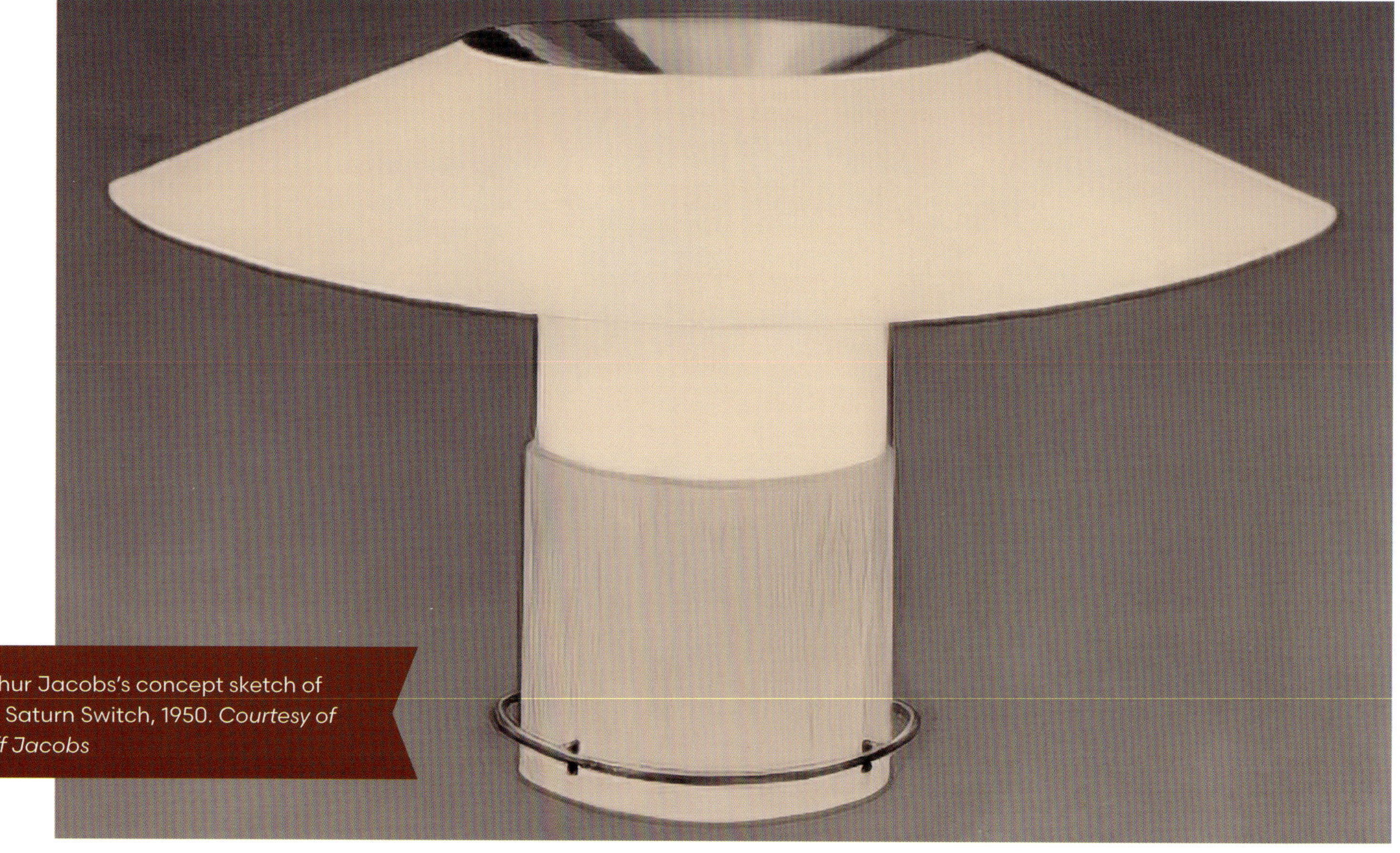

Arthur Jacobs's concept sketch of the Saturn Switch, 1950. *Courtesy of Jeff Jacobs*

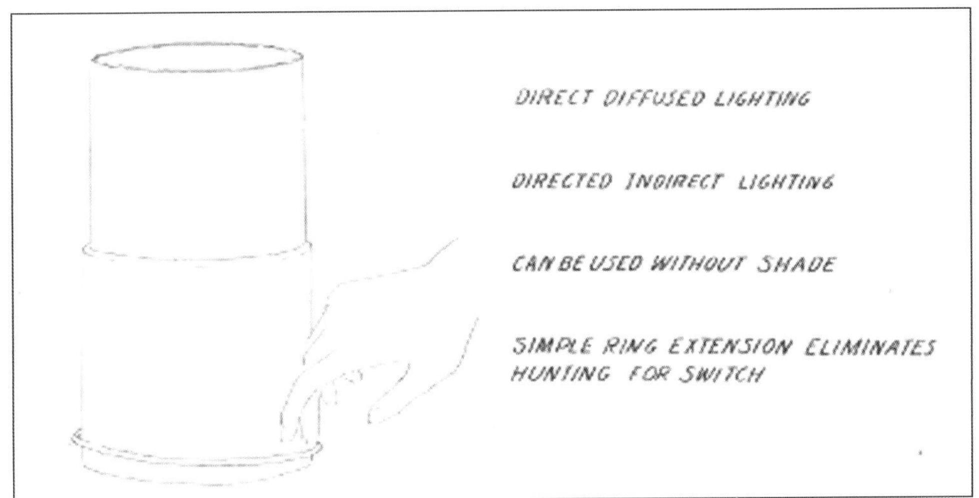

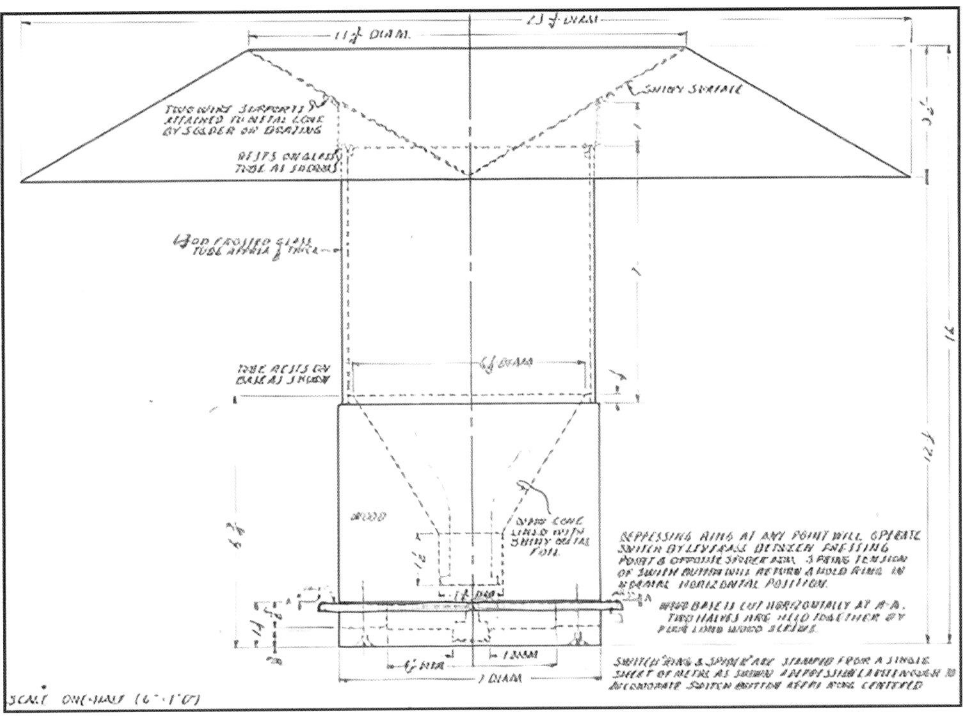

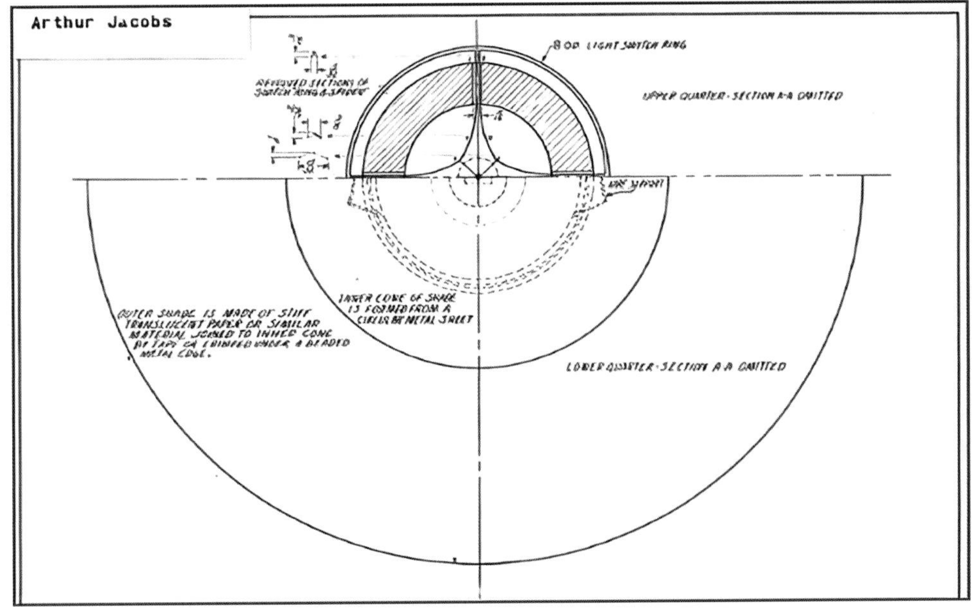

Courtesy of Jeff Jacobs

Standing at a gargantuan 49 inches, it was an awkwardly tall table lamp. Buyers found this to be an off-putting characteristic. Its massive stature eclipsed its surroundings, making blending quite difficult.

Coming off what Bernie felt was an embarrassing misreading of buyers' desires, he found himself receiving a bit of insult on top of this injury at a 1962 press conference at the opening of Merchandise Mart's International Home Furnishings Market in Chicago. Interior designers at this press conference showed up looking for a fight. The common thread among their abstract and sprawling complaints: There has been nothing new in the world of lighting in many years. Lawrence Peabody remarked that the newest offerings in lighting were a "profusion of strange shapes," and he went on to say that his New Hampshire home was lit mostly by candles, with the exception of two oil lamps, since none of the modern options were appealing to him. Gilbert Gray joined in the churlish chorus to refer to modern lamps as "the greatest abuse since the 1937 airflow Chrysler," describing them as "top-heavy titans on small end tables." Texas designer Roy F. Beal said that "most large lamps are distortions," and that manufacturers should consider implementing lower, easier-to-reach base switches. C. Eugene Stevenson, fellow of the American Institute of Interior Designers, chimed in to say that the newest lamps have "dull, hackneyed forms" and are not engineered for practical use. Bernie took the bait and snapped back at what he felt was a parade of out-of-touch self-importance. Referring to the retired Model 8550, he said, "To eliminate the problem of pulling on a light, we introduced a lamp with a plate in the base which you touched to turn on the light. The consumer didn't accept it, so we dropped it." In response to the "nothing new" charge, Bernie pointed to Modeline's vast innovation not only in lamp bases, but in switches, shade materials, and general styling. "Just what do you people want?" he asked the panel of designers. The only clear answer came from Peabody, who expressed his belief that more table lamps should be equipped with dimmer switches.

This final complaint concerning the lack of dimmer control switches among portable lamps was the only one that Bernie felt existed within the bounds of reality. Getting right to work on correcting this, Arthur Jacobs developed a functional dimmer control switch for certain table and floor model lamps for the summer of 1962. This rheostatic control dial was named

The home of Holly and Aaron Board, Sarasota, Florida. *Photographer Daniel Perales*

the Gradulite Switch, and consumers loved it. But when Bernie attended the press brunch at the opening day of Los Angeles Home Furnishings Mart's Summer Market, a group of interior designers were once again armed with a list of tall demands. As if reading from Lawrence Peabody's script, Adele Faulkner launched into a wholesale condemnation of modern lamp designs. "There has been little change in the lamp industry over the past fifty years," she said. "The industry is afraid to pioneer in an extremely competitive field." Not satisfied with Modeline's incorporation of dimmer switches on some of their models, she insisted that *all* portable lamps ought to have dimmers. Not stopping there, she also took aim at the lamp's power source, saying that no thought was being put into the design of unsightly cords that often ended up jumbled into a rubber band so as to avoid being a tripping hazard.

Bernie left the event scratching his head and wondering whether interior designers were paying any attention whatsoever to Modeline's responses to their past complaints. Nevertheless, he brought these concerns back to the design team. Some experimentation was done with adapting a functional, battery-powered lamp, but it was deemed impractical.

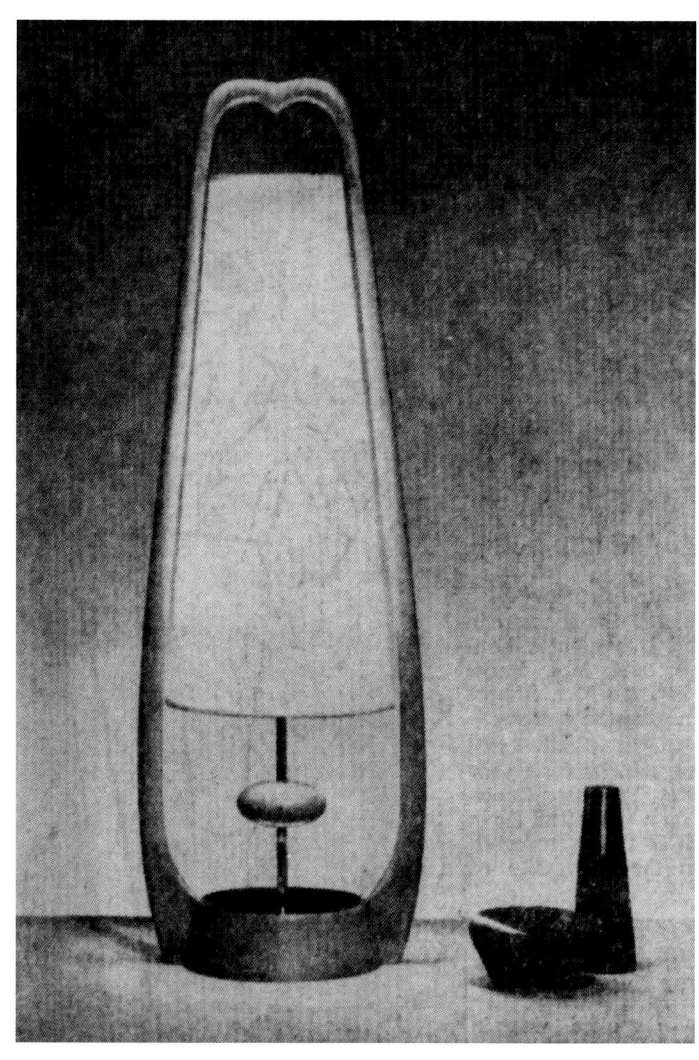

Arthur Jacobs's 1961 boudoir lamp, equipped with a saucer-shaped Modeliter switch. *Copyright Modeline Co.*

Arthur Jacobs's 1961 Checkerboard table lamp. *Copyright Modeline Co.*

An Arthur Jacobs-designed 43.5"
Model 1925 table lamp.
Photographer Paige Hood

The Elephant on the End Table

The gargantuan size of many Modeline table lamps was a polarizing feature from the time of their creation. The height of table lamps throughout the 1940s and up until the mid-1950s averaged around 30 inches, with taller exceptions closer to 36 inches. How then, and why, did 41-to-54-inch table lamps come to exist? Designers such as Lawrence Peabody bore more responsibility for the size trends of 1960s table lamps, in fact, than did the manufacturers of these goliaths. The age of modern brought with it the popularity of reclined, lazy seating. A position that only a decade prior might have been viewed as overly informal for a living room became the preference of many young people by the mid-1950s. Sofa designs and construction subsequently became lower to the ground, and lounge chairs were often created in a permanently reclined position. And what about that cocktail? The whole idea of entertaining in comfort risked being compromised if one needed to sit up and stretch simply to take a sip of his Tom Collins or set down the Sunday paper. The solution was simple: Designers created shorter end tables. Tables that, decades prior, stood at 25 or more inches tall shrunk to an average of 20 inches to accommodate this relaxed position. Something that did not change, however, was the ideal floor-to-bulb distance among portable lamps for the creation of an aesthetically pleasing living space. Statement lamps that would have been 36 inches became locked in an evolutionary arms race with the shrinking chairs and tables. Overall height shot up, and switch placement, at least for Modeline of California, came down. The result was a table lamp that was, by early 1950s standards, indistinguishable in stature from the floor lamps of the previous decade.

The Garrison House, Birmingham, Alabama. *Photographer Liesa Cole*

An Arthur Jacobs–designed torchiere table lamp.
Photographer Libby Danforth

A saucer Modeliter-equipped table lamp pair by Arthur Jacobs. *Photographer Libby Danforth*

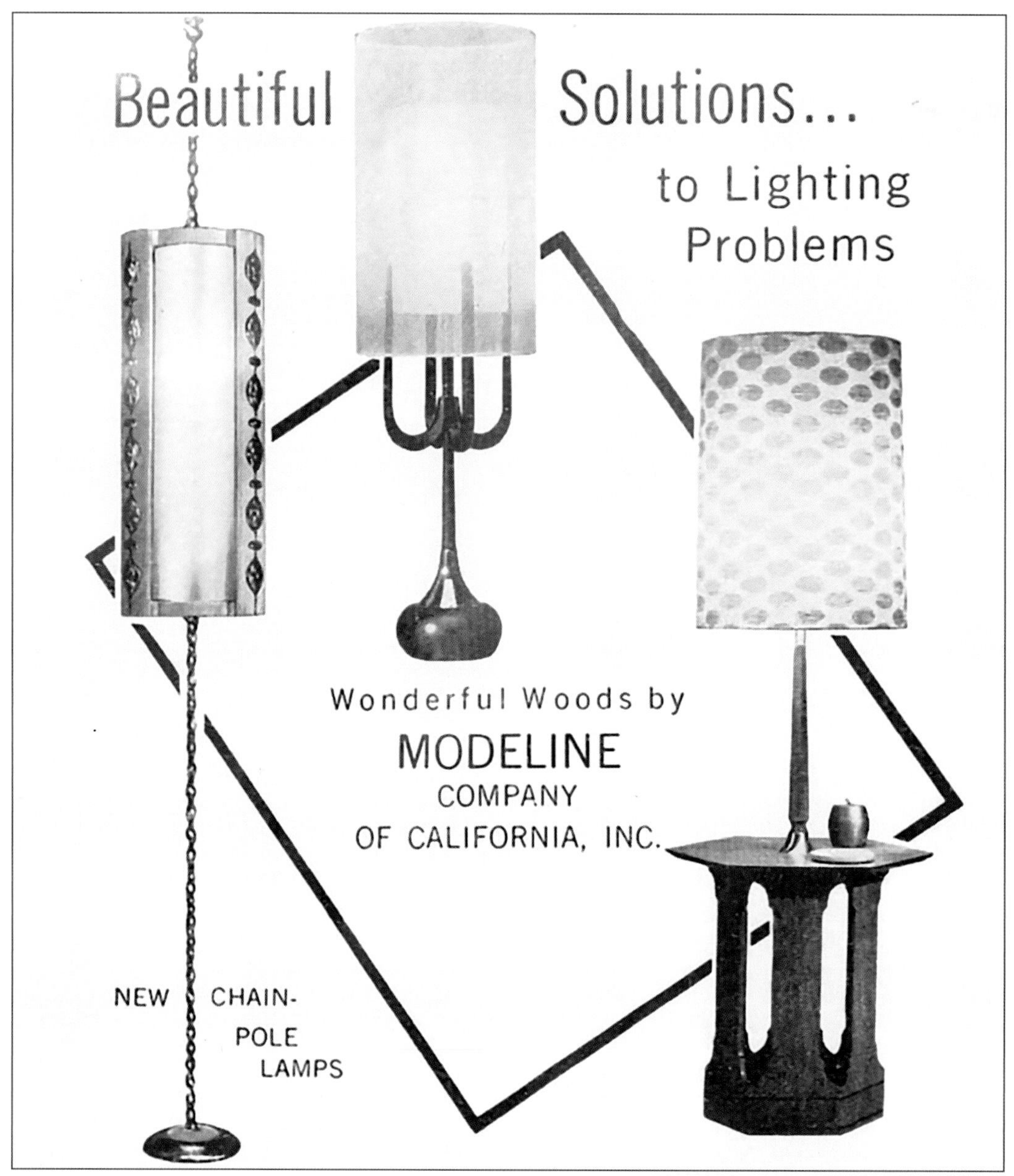

Copyright Modeline Co.

Despite the harsh and arguably ill-placed criticism of interior designers, Modeline had never been in better standing. The brand had become synonymous with luxury and refined taste by the early 1960s, but there was one great territory left to conquer—the ceiling. Trends toward modernism in architecture were continuing, so Bernie wanted the design team to develop ceiling fixtures that would create the same aesthetic cohesion that Modeline had created with their korina table and floor lamps. After a few meetings to explore what direction to take with these new lamps, Haywood, Jacobs, and Keal divvied up the project. Arthur Jacobs focused on chain lamps, since he found that it would be relatively easy work to adapt some of his table lamp designs into chain lamp variants. This would allow him to continue devoting his time to the projects that he could already count on being successful. Jack Haywood undertook the design of Modeline's chandeliers. He had created a few designs in the past for Tony Hill as well as several others in his home workshop, so this was a project for which he felt very qualified. John Keal, in addition to contributing several chain lamps, designed what was arguably Modeline's most fascinating creation of 1962—the chain pole.

John Keal's chain pole lamp.
Photographer Paige Hood

Copyright Modeline Co.

The chain pole was a marriage of Theophile Stiffel's invention the "lampole" and a hanging chain lamp. It solved the problem of ceiling height that plagued the pole lamp market, which was limited in most cases to 8- and 9-foot-ceiling compatibility. The chain pole did not rely on spring tension to stand upright. Rather, it let gravity do all the work. It also did not need to route an unsightly chain and cord across the ceiling and down the wall like a chain lamp, since the power was supplied from the weighted base rather than from the top. Bernie's decision not to include traditional pole lamps among Modeline's offerings was inspired by two factors. The first of these was the fact that the construction of a pole lamp relied so heavily on a metal center standard that the lamps would likely have lost the Modeline feel of being constructed primarily from wood. The second factor, and personally the most important to him, was that Theophile Stiffel was a friend, and he was involved in an ongoing, expensive lawsuit against Sears & Roebuck. This case, which ultimately ended in a United States Supreme Court decision against Stiffel, nearly bankrupted Stiffel Lamp Company. Bernie did not see a good reason to contribute to the wounds of a friend, and he decided that Modeline, unlike its competitors, would never offer a tension pole lamp of any kind.

The Garrison House, Birmingham, Alabama. *Photographer Liesa Cole*

A 1962 John Keal–designed chain lamp. *Photographer Libby Danforth*

Opposite: The Ferrell House, Chattanooga, Tennessee. *Photographer Libby Danforth*

A 1962 Jack Haywood–designed chandelier.
Photographer Paige Hood

A 1963 Arthur Jacobs–designed chandelier.
Photographer Libby Danforth

CALIFORNIA INTERIORS

A mid-1960s Jack Haywood-designed chain lamp table. The Ferrell House, Chattanooga, Tennessee. *Photographer Libby Danforth*

A 1962 Arthur Jacobs–designed chain lamp.
Photographer Libby Danforth

A 1963 Arthur Jacobs–designed chain lamp.
Photographer Libby Danforth

A 1963 John Keal-designed chain lamp. The Ferrell House, Chattanooga, Tennessee. *Photographer Libby Danforth*

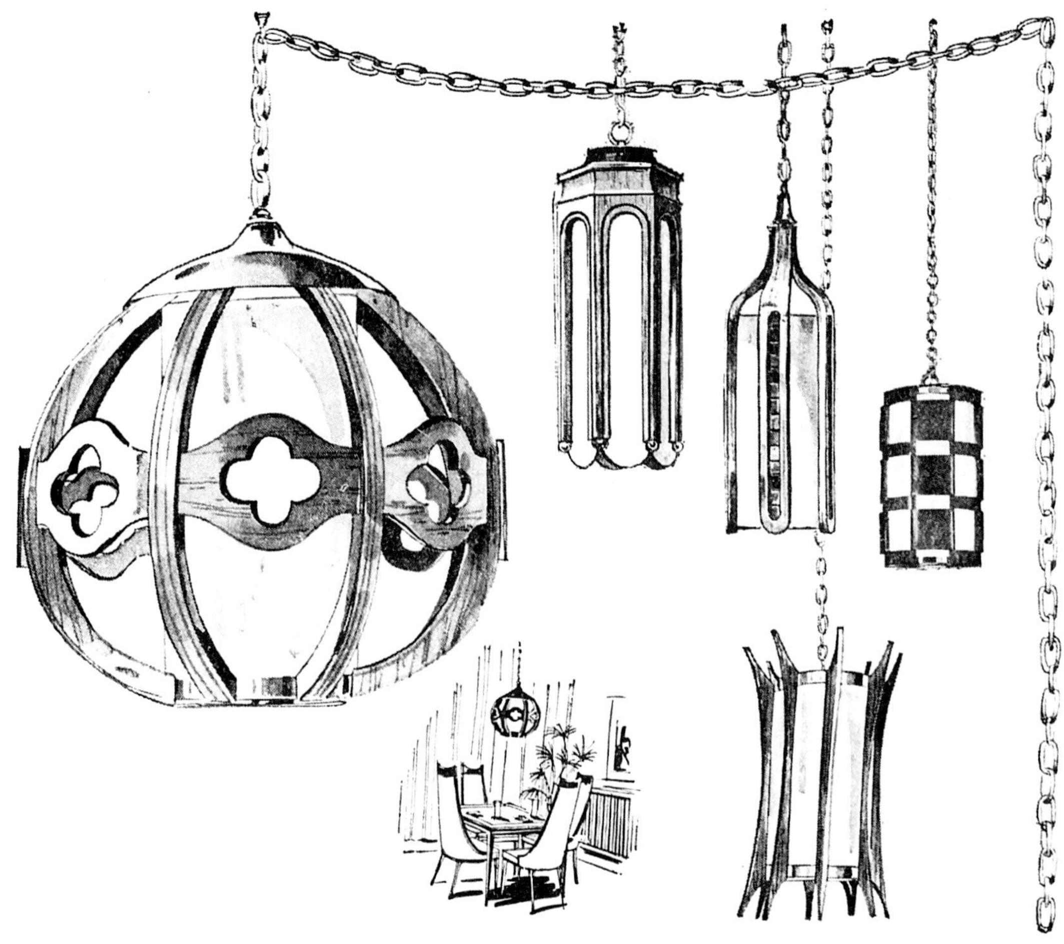

Copyright Modeline Co.

Modeline's step into the world of ceiling lights became their largest success to date. Wasting no time, they offered forty-eight chain lamps, eighteen chandeliers, four chain pole lamps, and thirty pendant lights in the 1962 catalog alone. With several years in the model home, hotel, and motel business under their belt, selling these fixtures in large volumes and getting them out in front of potential buyers proved to be easy work. Within only a few months of their initial release, these ceiling lights were being installed into new hotel and motel construction across the Midwest and East Coast. The self-perpetuating machine of exposure marketing was in full swing, and American consumers couldn't get enough. The wide range of new ceiling lights would have been an impressive enough showing for 1962, but these also came with the debut of 196 new floor and table lamp models by Arthur Jacobs, Jack Haywood, John Keal, Bill Dorff, John Caldwell, and Byron Botker.

The lobby of the Grand Motel in Myrtle Beach, South Carolina, outfitted with Modeline pendant lights, 1963.
Courtesy of Getty Images

A 1963 John Keal–designed pendant light.
Photographer Paige Hood

A 1962 John Keal-designed pendant light.
Photographer Paige Hood

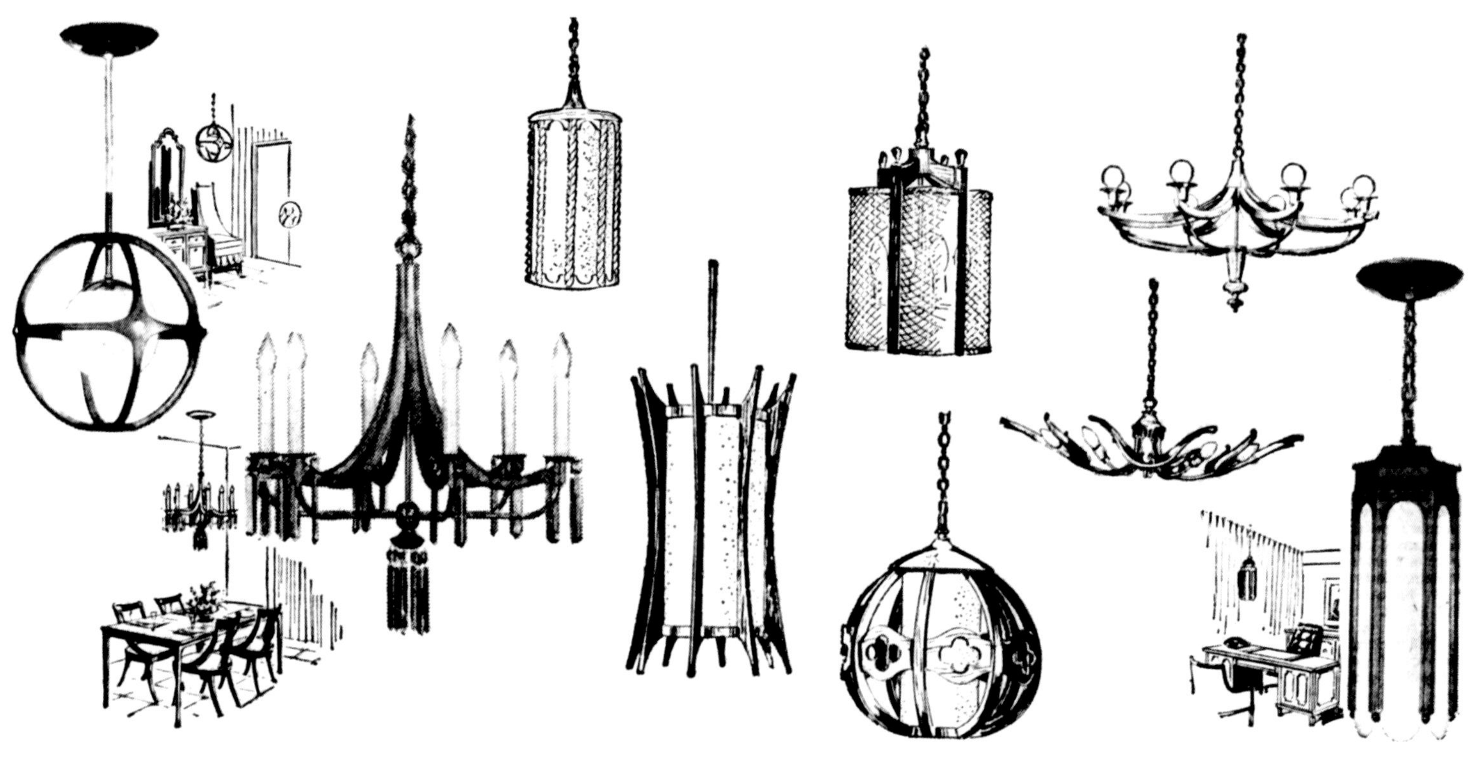

Copyright Modeline Co.

The love affair between American consumers and Modeline ceiling lights was ablaze, with Modeline fulfilling orders in just enough time for dealers to sell out again. They were a smash hit. That is, with one exception—Jack Haywood's chandeliers. These chandeliers were striking in appearance and undeniably attractive, but a bit primitive, especially for Haywood. Jack had initially presented his modern designs to Keal, but Keal insisted that chandelier buyers were not ready to embrace a fully modern chandelier. Haywood disagreed, but Keal ultimately won out. John modified many of Haywood's initial designs and moved forward on production. Too modern for traditional buyers and too traditional for modern buyers, these designs failed to connect to the market. Jack Haywood found this to be quite disheartening, and he did not hesitate to share his views on this matter to the press, saying, "I am disappointed in the reluctance of manufacturers to accept a truly contemporary chandelier. Although some elegant crystal chandeliers do seem to complement some contemporary dining furniture rather well, it is my opinion that a well-designed contemporary piece, with clean, uncluttered lines, could be just as elegant and much more appropriate with this furniture. Such a chandelier, with no concession to traditional motifs, would answer a need for such lighting with the furniture that is so pure as to be completely at odds with the traditional crystal chandeliers." If ever there was a doubt about the degree to which Bernie Roberts respected his employees, complaining about one's superiors in the *Los Angeles Times* on Friday and still having a job on Monday was, to put it mildly, not typical.

A 1962 Arthur Jacobs–designed chain lamp.
Photographer Paige Hood

Modeline sales manager Joe Stock (*right*) confirms an order of chain lamps for Jack Brandwein (*center*) of Brandwein Furniture, Sacramento, California. *Copyright Modeline Co.*

While John Keal may have overshot his critique of Jack Haywood's chandeliers, he was correct in his observation that there was a large portion of buyers who were not yet completely ready to embrace modern design. The common criticisms of modern styling, often coming from the older generation, were that modern designs were cold, stark, and stiff. In contrast to their art nouveau and art deco ancestors, these criticisms made sense. There was very little transition time between the maximalist designs of the Gatsby era and the minimalism of early modernism. Even the atomic designs of the 1940s were considerably more animated than their modern descendants. To reach these hesitant buyers, Modeline introduced what they called the "soft modern" look in 1963. The feel of soft modern was a more curvaceous, lively version of modernism that, while maintaining a clearly modern design, strayed away from 90-degree angles and straight lines and relied more on gently rounded contours.

A "soft modern" buffet lamp by Arthur Jacobs. *Photographer Paige Hood*

An early-1960s floor lamp by Arthur Jacobs.
Photographer Paige Hood

An early-1960s floor lamp by Arthur Jacobs. *Photographer Paige Hood*

A mid-1960s Jack Haywood–designed chain lamp. *Photographer Libby Danforth*

The home of Laura Taylor and Chelsea Bailey, Nashville, Tennessee. *Photographer Libby Danforth*

Copyright Modeline Co.

In light of the recent demands from interior designers for lower, more-convenient lamp switches, Bernie made the decision to bring the Saturn Switch–equipped models back into rotation. Arthur Jacobs, who was proud of the lamp and stood to profit from its sales, was pleased with this decision. Jack Haywood was not. He did not have anything against Jacobs or the Saturn Switch, but he felt that kowtowing to interior designers, who had not done much in recent years to help promote Modeline lamps to buyers, was a mistake. Nevertheless, John Keal, Arthur Jacobs, and Bernie Roberts all agreed that offering the Saturn Switch could not do anything to hurt the brand. The Saturn Switch was reissued in the fall 1964 catalog. While it never achieved the sales numbers that the Modeliter-equipped lamps did, the sales of the mid-1960s reissue were much stronger than they were upon its initial release. Modeline had not been wrong about this lamp; they had only been too early. Closing this gap between the lamp that buyers were accustomed to and the lamp that buyers needed would have otherwise been the role of interior designers if not for their recent referendum against modern lighting. This remained a sticking point for Bernie, who felt strongly that interior designers—not Modeline—had failed to perceive and respond to their clients' needs in new switch designs and modern lamps in general.

Sadly, the two years of sparring with interior designers would not be the last of Modeline's mid-1960s woes. Straying a bit further from modern design, John Keal introduced a line of twelve Spanish-inspired lamps. The thinking behind this line was to increase Modeline's sales on the West Coast by leaning into California's Spanish heritage. Sales of the 1950s and early 1960s had become concentrated east of the Mississippi River. The unique perk and slight conflict of interest that came with being both a designer and the design director was that John Keal's designs were approved at his own discretion and marketed more heavily than the designs of others at Modeline. But even after months of heavy advertising and presentation at furniture markets, the Spanish lamps fell flat. Modern buyers were not interested and were skeptical of the ads that suggested that they would blend easily with a modern aesthetic. Spanish-design buyers tended to opt for wrought iron and glass lamps. Decorators considered them overly antiquated and too ornate for current tastes.

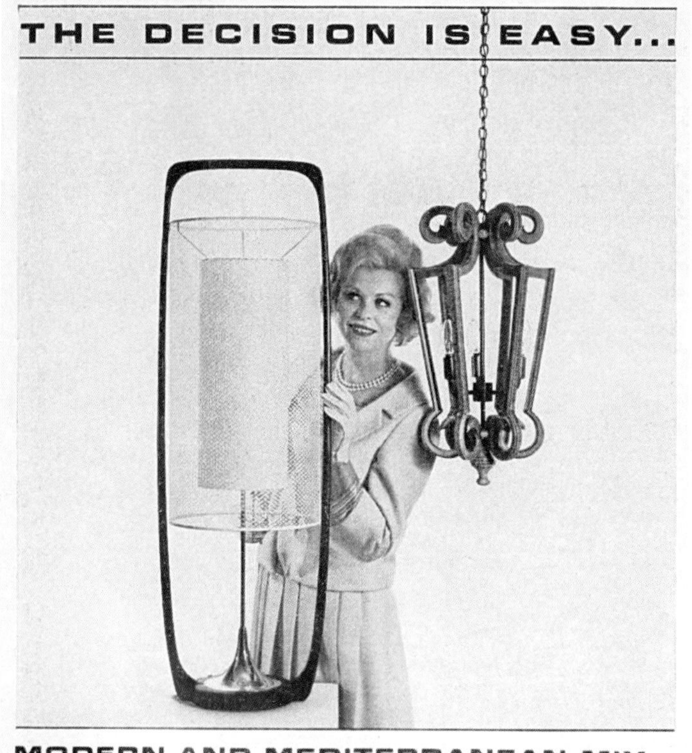

Ben Gurule. *Copyright Modeline Co.*

Looking to turn this bit of bad luck around, Bernie and Esther took an inspiration-seeking vacation to Hong Kong. Bernie brought photographs and souvenirs to his designers, praising the blending of pagoda and modern architecture of East Asia. Each designer incorporated elements of this into some of their 1964 designs, with John Keal being the first to return with a series of pagoda-inspired floor, table, and hanging lamps.

Of the many wonders of the Far East, Bernie was most fascinated with the folded-paper art of Zhezhi. He felt that something like this could be incorporated into Modeline's shade design. Worrying that this was outside Modeline's current capabilities, he sought the help of a folded-paper artist who was just beginning to make a buzz around Los Angeles—Ben Gurule. Outside of his art, Ben and his wife, Kay, were Mexican American activists who worked with the American Civil Liberties Union on reforming what they felt was an anti-Hispanic bias in the California public school system. While Bernie hired all types of individuals with all sorts of different political dispositions, he was drawn to like-minded people and wanted as many of them at Modeline as he could find. Gurule was the perfect fit both in terms of capability and ideals. In December 1964, Gurule began working on a series of folded-paper hanging lamps that would create a "lighted Zhezhi" appearance. The prototypes of these lamps were impressively unique from anything available at the time. Paper did not, in the end, serve as a suitable material for construction, since it was too prone to denting and tearing and it failed to support its own weight effectively. A thin polyvinyl chloride (PVC) wound up being the ideal material, since it was many times stronger than paper, but it wasn't too heavy to hang.

A pagoda-inspired floor and hanging lamp by John Keal.
Photographer Libby Danforth

One of Ben Gurule's Facet Lights. *Copyright Modeline Co.*

This thin PVC material allowed Gurule to design these lights with an invisible, built-in support system that he called "Acruflexive Support." This kept his lights free from wood or metal reinforcement, causing them to evoke the same amount of awe and wonder that Modeline had created with their impossibly delicate, sculpted-wood forms. In every other sense, these lights were extremely unlike Modeline lamps. No wooden bases, no creative switches, and no dimensional shades. Fearing that there would be confusion among consumers about the direction that Modeline was headed, Bernie felt that it would be best to create a degree of separation between Gurule's folded lights and the sculpted-wood lamps. This new line of lamps—Facet Lights—would be sold under the new Modeline subsidiary Q Lighting Division. Q Lighting would serve as a canary in the coal mine, testing out the most-ambitious and most-unusual designs before putting them into mass production under the Modeline brand.

When the time came to debut Facet Lights, the praise was abounding. Henry Dreyfuss, who was something of a design monarch at the time, called Ben Gurule the "Leonardo da Vinci of folded paper." Gurule was also given an award for design excellence by the Pasadena Art Museum. Facet Lights were displayed in several California trade shows and art museums, and everywhere they went the accolades followed. Representatives from Macy's saw these lights at Carson, Pirie, and Scott's California Design and California Products show and insisted that Bernie come in to discuss distribution at their department stores. Another year of refinement followed, and in the spring of 1966 these lights were on display at Modeline's permanent showrooms as well as select dealers and Macy's department stores.

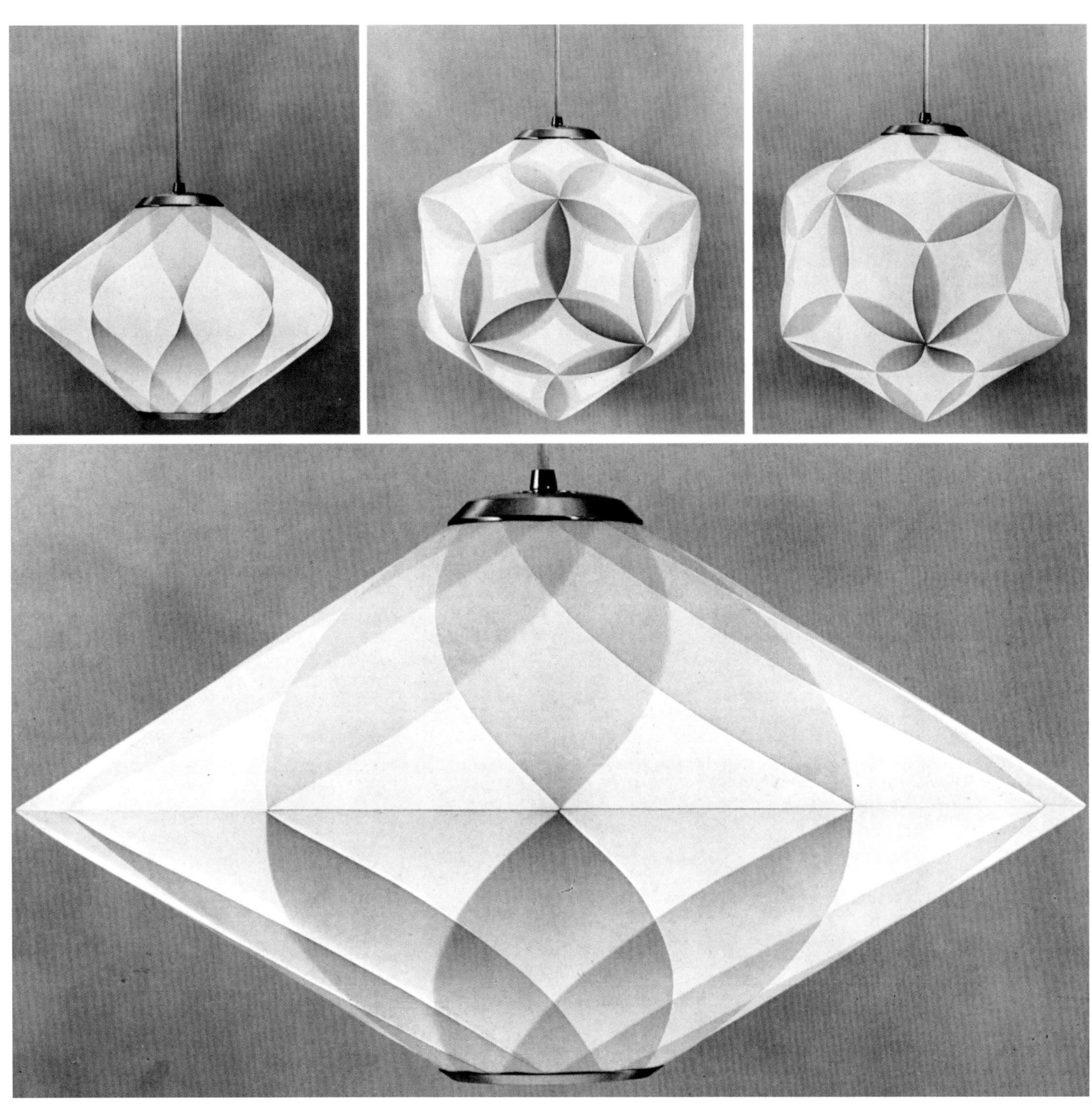

facet light

Be first with the newest, soundest and most beautiful lighting invention in years. Patented construction needs no interior framework. Newly-perfected support system uses durable translucent plastic. U.L. approved. Shade detaches easily for cleaning and for changing bulb. Created in California by Ben Gurule. Recognized for design excellence by Pasadena Art Museum in commercial and residential class. Nine classic designs. Unprecedented beauty, shapes and lighting quality for decorative or functional illumination. Moderately priced. Nationally distributed. Write for catalog & information. **TERRITORIES OPEN.** Contact **Q LIGHTING,** a division of Modeline Co. of Calif., Inc. 110 No. Beaudry · Los Angeles, Calif. 90012 · (213) MA 4-8312 · Since 1945

Copyright Modeline Co.

A 1965 magazine rack floor lamp, designed by Bill Dorff. *Copyright Modeline Co.*

After two years of building momentum, by the end of 1966, Modeline had a clear picture of the sales numbers on the Facet Lights. They were abysmal. Despite being the longest and most costly research-and-development process at Modeline, the lights looked cheaply made to most consumers. The folded vinyl appeared to be brittle, and it was suspected of lacking longevity. The white forms were also difficult to match with 1966 interiors. Modeline, a company praised for being ahead of its time, had in this instance overestimated the willingness of buyers to embrace a new style of lighting. Some Facet Lights remained in production for the following three years, and some of them were adapted to be used as shades for wood-based lamps. This would ultimately slow to a complete stop by 1969 and be the last word from Ben Gurule at Modeline.

This misjudgment of the market introduced a bit of panic in Bernie Roberts. Sales at the firm were strong, but the lamps that were selling were mostly early 1960s designs. There was no clear data to determine what the lamps of late 1960s interiors ought to look like. A chasm had formed between the preferences of buyers and the recommendations of interior designers. The lamps that buyers adored—the modern designs of the late 1950s through 1964, interior designers picked apart. The lamps that interior designers and design critics adored—the Facet Lights, buyers had no use for. This jolt sent Bernie, along with Arthur Jacobs, Jack Haywood, and John Keal, back to the drawing board to determine what the spirit of Modeline would be for the late 1960s.

An Arthur Jacobs floor and table lamp, each equipped with the Gradulite dimmer control. *Photographer Libby Danforth*

The Garrison House, Birmingham, Alabama.
Photographer Liesa Cole

A John Keal-designed floor lamp with a molded fabric shade.
Photographer Libby Danforth

CHAPTER 8

The Space Age

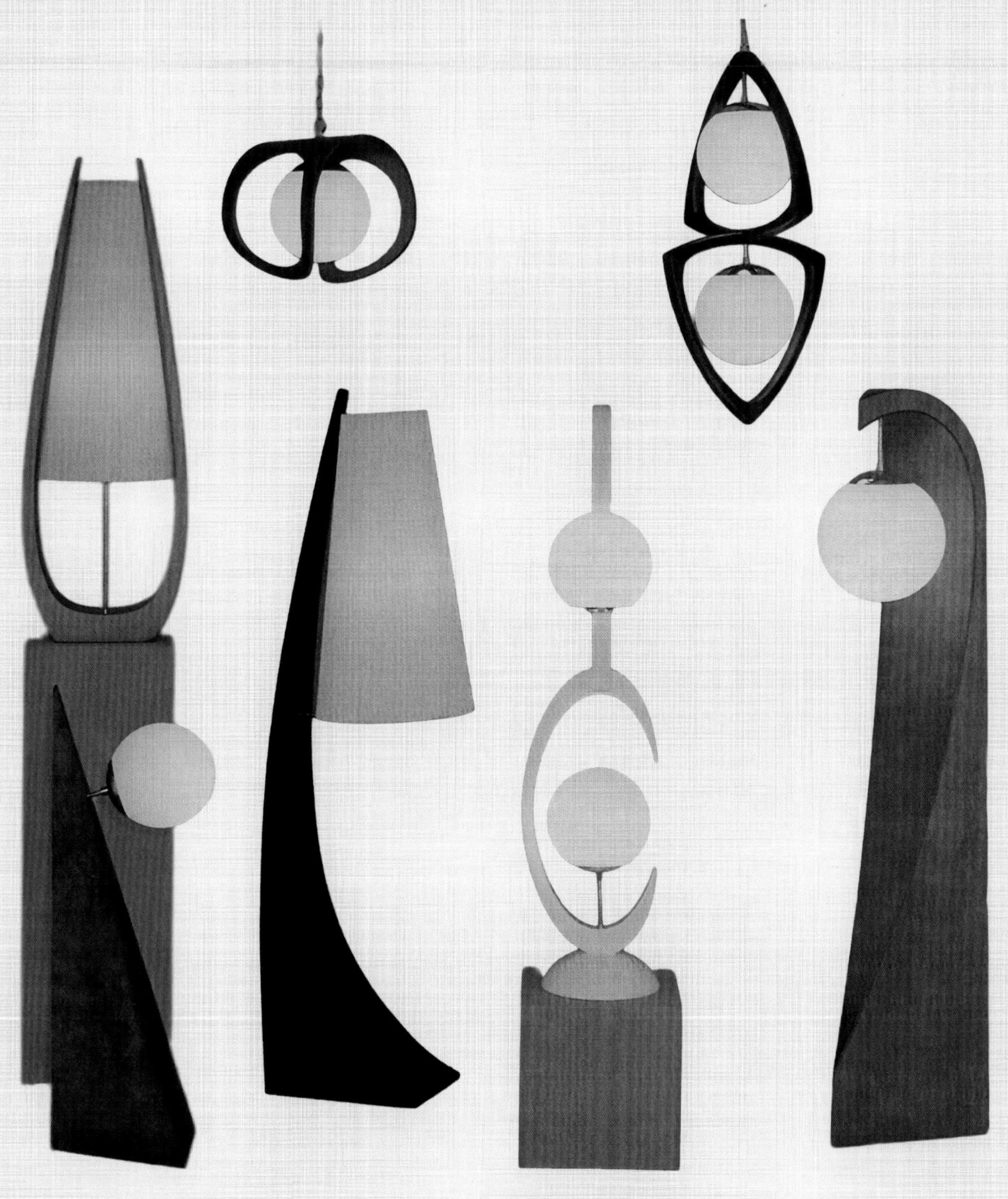

With the space race at full throttle and the first images taken from another celestial body reaching Earth, the average American was being inundated with new and alien visions that had previously been depicted only within the realm of science fiction. The effect that this had on tastes in furniture and interior lighting was immediate and profound. While wood was still the primary build material among all case goods manufacturers, experimental new design choices were being made that would bring the aesthetic of the final frontier into American homes. Smoked glass, plastics, chrome accents, and solid-color enamels were quickly gaining popularity. Modeline sought to be the first firm to offer lighting that would complement this new style. In a break from tradition, which generally had Arthur Jacobs conceptualizing the themes of the new model collections, Bernie asked Jack Haywood if he would lead the way into this new territory. Haywood was Modeline's futurist—a true master at pushing modern design to its next evolutionary stage. The idea for the Modeline lamps of the late 1960s would be to offer something that would be a continuation of modernism, but with some more technologically influenced elements.

LIGHT AND SHADE

Sculptural treatment of both the wood frame and pleated fabric shade makes this 22-inch-tall hanging lamp by Modeline a striking source of illumination in any room setting

Pleated fabric

Copyright Modeline Co.

The first idea, which Haywood created in his home workshop and presented to Jacobs and Keal in November 1966, was a brand-new type of lampshade: pleated and molded, plastic-backed fabric lampshades that offered excellent light diffusion without any need for a new or proprietary material. Simply by holding their complex forms, which was accomplished by heat-pressing and mounting this material into preformed wooden grooves, these shades created a play between the light source and the shadow cast by protrusions in the shade. This canceled out the hotspots and glare that Modeline had strived so hard to avoid in their previous shade innovations.

Copyright Modeline Co.

A line of forty table lamps, floor lamps, and chain lamps debuted at the Los Angeles Furniture Mart Summer Market in 1967. In a moment that had been five years in the making, the praises of interior designers could be heard once again. Pleated and molded fabric shades embodied the feel of 1967. Soft, warm walnut tones in perfect contrast with eggshell and cream linette fabric, formed into impossibly complex shapes, accomplished exactly what Modeline needed them to in that moment. Modeline's profitability had not been in serious question since the early 1950s, but the perpetual reintroduction of the brand as the most relevant manufacturer of contemporary lighting was not something that could have been established once and for all. As preferences changed, the brand had to change. For Modeline's status as a pioneer and a maverick to remain as true as it was when Bernie Roberts created his own molded Sofglo lampshades, no time could be wasted in perceiving the needs of buyers and understanding societal changes and their implications on future design trends. Pleated fabric accomplished exactly that.

Opposite: An Arthur Jacobs–designed chain lamp with a pleated fabric shade. *Photographer Paige Hood*

A John Keal–designed table lamp with a molded fabric shade. *Photographer Paige Hood*

A John Keal-designed floor lamp
with a molded fabric shade.
Photographer Libby Danforth

Copyright Modeline Co.

With Jack Haywood seated front and center at Modeline's innovation game, Arthur Jacobs placed his focus on adapting his lamp designs to the changing buyers' preferences rather than creating new switch options. The Gradulite dimmer, by 1967, was available on 390 unique models, and that number was growing. For all the interior designers' misplaced complaints, they appeared to be correct about one of them—buyers loved a dimmer control. Among Jacobs's newest designs was a table lamp and corresponding chain lamp that were inspired by the art of Piet Mondrian, with a tip of the hat to Frank Lloyd Wright. At a gargantuan 40 inches tall by 10 inches wide, the dimmer was clearly the only concession that Jacobs intended to make to the list of demands that had been presented by decorators. While the warm, walnut finish on korina was still present, it broke free in many other ways from Jacobs's 1950s and early 1960s designs. The bright-turquoise, gold, and ocean-blue polyester inserts were distinct from the earth tones of the earlier models. The geometric forms also lent to a less natural feel in exchange for one that was unapologetically artistic.

John Keal's few contributions for 1967 were equally abnormal in light of his previous designs. In addition to a reintroduction of six new Spanish-style lamps and the Skyscraper floor lamp, he created his first nonlighted pieces for Modeline. At the request of Shirley and Esther Roberts, who were heavy cigarette smokers, Keal created a line of standing ashtrays in Modeline's classic korina-and-brass style.

Hate those ashes?

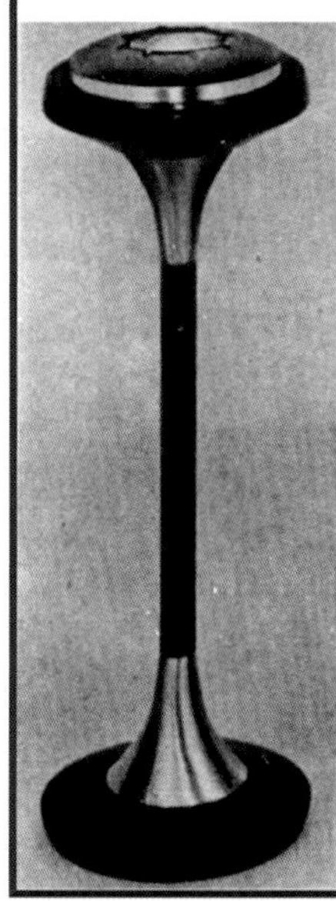

If your family includes members who smoke—be it cigars, a pipe or cigarettes — then you know the crying need for ashtrays that are ample as well as decorative. Here are two well-designed smoking stands from a new line styled by John Keal for Modeline of California. Wood finishes are walnut or black; metal finishes are satin brass or satin chrome. The glass liner that fits into the tray is easily removed for cleaning. Available at Alfred Dunhill, Beverly Hills.

Copyright Modeline Co.

Opposite: Arthur Jacobs's Mondrian-style table lamps. *Photographer Libby Danforth*

The Ferrell House, Chattanooga, Tennessee.
Photographer Libby Danforth

John Keal's "Skyscraper" floor lamp.
Photographer Libby Danforth

An Arthur Jacobs–designed, Modeliter-equipped room divider. *Photographer Libby Danforth*

New Lamps Called 'Lighted Furniture'

Modeline of California, manufacturer of sculptured wood lamps, is showing its newest collection of "lighted furniture" with a total contemporary felling in keeping with today's predominating decorator trend.

Trade authorities are using "lighted furniture" to describe Modeline lamps because of their unusual contemporary beauty, function, materials and fine illumination, offering more than the properties of normal lamps.

California designers Arthur Jacobs and Jack Haywood are responsible for the 30 modern numbers being introduced by Modeline.

Copyright Modeline Co.

Another new development, as Modeline breached the uncharted territory of the late 1960s, was the intermingling of styles among the big three designers. Up until this point, the defining lines between the work of each individual designer were clear enough that one with enough exposure to their work could correctly identify the creator of a particular lamp with relative ease. After 1966, this became a bit more complex. Arthur Jacobs created several Spanish-style lamps that were right at home among Keal's designs. Jacobs and Keal both used Haywood's pleated fabric shades on several of their new offerings. Haywood implemented Jacobs's fluted plastic shade material, and all three used Ben Gurule's Acruflexive shades, perhaps so as to give Gurule a proper send-off. One feature that remained consistent, however, was the use of Arthur Jacobs's specialty switches. In no instance did the Modeliter, Mercury Switch, or Saturn Switch appear on any lamp design that did not originate with Arthur Jacobs. This was not for lack of willingness on the part of Arthur Jacobs, who freely offered the implementation of his switches to the other designers. John Keal and Jack Haywood carried a tremendous amount of reverence for Jacobs's innovations, though, and did not feel that confusing buyers on their origin would have been respectful.

Modeline's venture into the new look in modern lighting landed tremendously well among decorators and buyers alike. The new models of 1967 launched Modeline to an all-time high in monthly sales. As the firm reemerged as the lighting company most well suited to meet the needs of buyers, Bernie Roberts and John Keal seized the opportunity to apply a bit of pressure to the design team. Bernie made a push to his designers to close out the 1960s with something that would dazzle decorators and allure buyers, something new and monumental that could not easily be replicated by any other firm. A series of lamps that would serve as a proud bookend to everything Modeline had accomplished so far—to usher in a new age in lighting. Arthur Jacobs brought his new geometric style, and Jack Haywood contributed his concepts of lighted room dividers. The result was a totally novel idea: Lighted Furniture. Lighted Furniture was a series of illuminated shelves and room dividers that were equal parts lighting and furniture. They were dainty and sleek in the way that the more successful mid-1950s Arthur Jacobs models had been, but square and geometric to create a style that was perfect for the direction that modern design was headed. They also had the added benefit of making Modeline at least partially immune from the growing fears of an economic downturn, as they captured a bit of the case goods market.

Opposite: Model 7120 floor lamp, designed by Bill Dorff. *Copyright Modeline Co.*

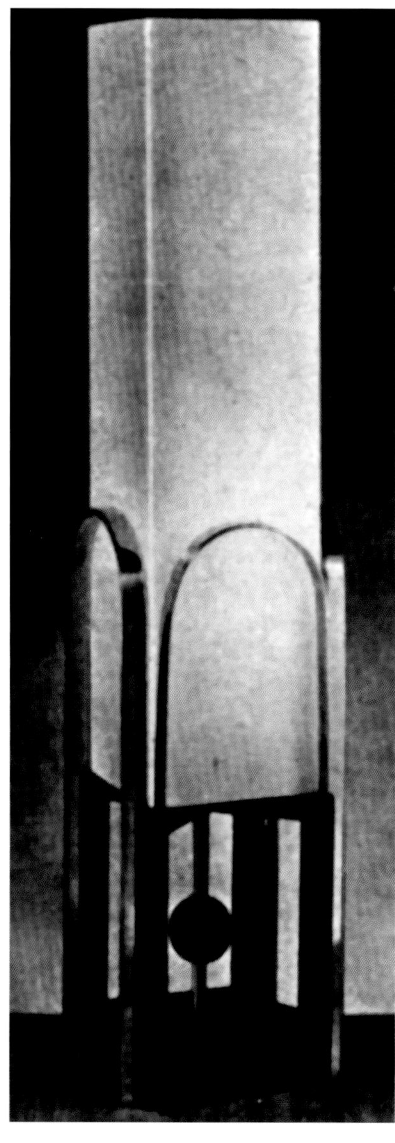

Copyright Modeline Co.

As Modeline made the necessary adaptations to this more geometric, late 1960s style, its mechanical mainstay—the Modeliter—evolved along with it. Arthur Jacobs's new designs for 1968 included several new versions of the wooden switch that included a rectangle, a sphere, a diamond, and an acorn shape. The Modeliter had been an instantly recognizable feature of so many Arthur Jacobs designs for so many years, and its imposters continued to abound. From Philadelphia to Yugoslavia, nearly every one of the Modeline copycat firms offered their own spin on the switch. Jacobs maintained that the rampant replication of the Modeliter was a testament to its usefulness and charm, and that there needn't be any effort to stop the many impersonators.

In addition to the new Modeliter varieties, shades were adapting at an equally impressive rate. A rectangular, open-weave dimensional shade, a gold webbing laminated over fiberglass shade, and a formed Plexiglas shade (supplied by Rohm & Haas) were new for '68. The acrylic shade quickly proved to be the most popular new offering. Using this sales data to predict the trends of 1969, the designers began to incorporate Plexiglas into nearly half of all new models for the 1969 catalog.

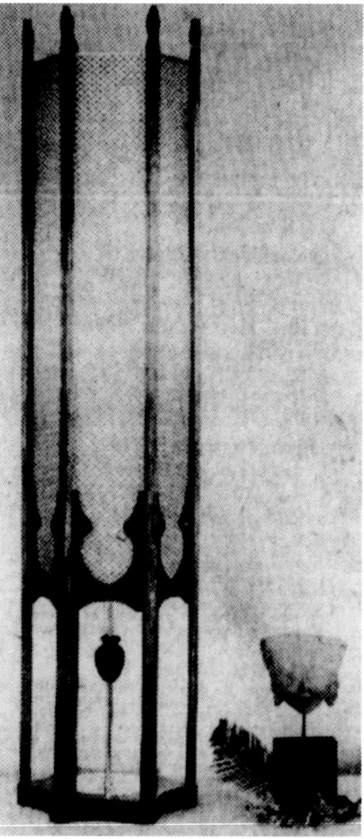

The Jack Haywood–designed "Slices of Light" table lamp. *Photographer Paige Hood*

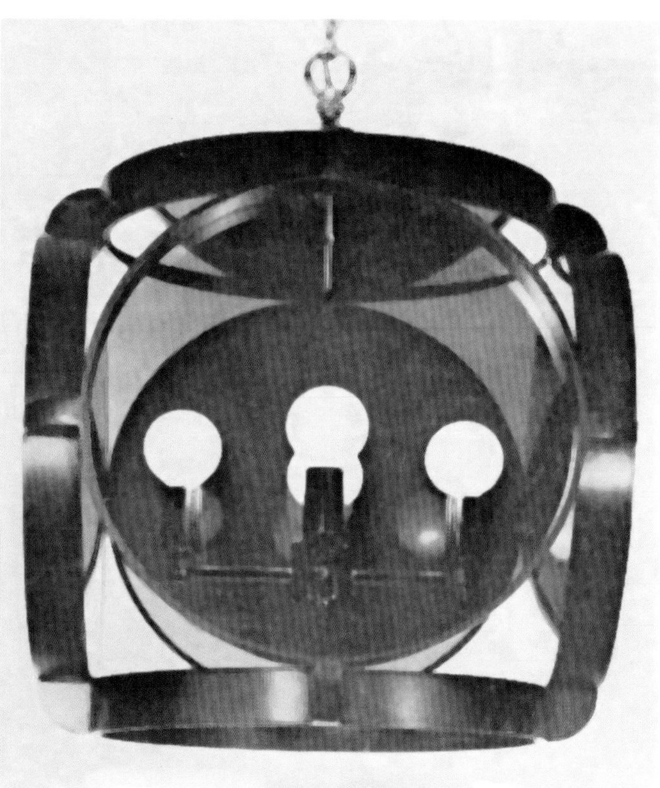

Copyright Modeline Co.

Modeline's implementation of this uniquely late 1960s mixed media—the blending of wood and acrylic—captured a new generation of buyers. The style did not connect terribly well with the older demographic or the modern buyers of the early 1960s, but it was a smash hit among buyers in their twenties. Not unlike what Modeline had experienced with the initial release of the Model 1545, the smoked acrylic look swept through the offerings of manufacturers across the country. The trinity of strong sales, rave reviews, and no shortage of copycats served as the confirmation that Bernie was looking for to enthusiastically embrace this new direction. He was always seeking to preserve the autonomy of the buyer, so acrylic panels were offered in smoke, yellow, red, white, and clear options. Several designs also implemented chrome trim to add an extra element of futurism. The shift away from fabric shades was also a distinct trend for 1969, with several of the new models lacking

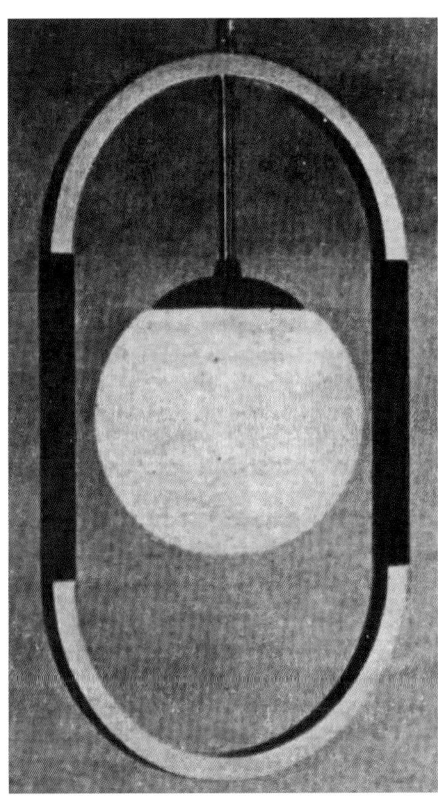

any kind of traditional lampshade in exchange for the satin glass "Moon Globe." Also new for 1969 was an array of "wet look" gloss polyester finish options in red, orange, avocado, lemon, and white with matching opaque shades. For a company that was founded on the throwing off of tradition and the embracing of new ideas, Modeline had spent nearly twenty-five years creating many traditions of their own. This Jack Haywood–led expedition into the final frontier of lighting proved once again that Modeline was not out of tricks. The pioneering spirit of California defined this brand, and there was no design or idea that could not be exchanged at any moment for a better one. The acrylics, exposed bulbs, glass globes, chrome trim, and vibrant new colors would have one believing that Modeline was founded during and for the space age. Not even for a moment did the brand insist that young buyers accept the lamps of the 1950s, but Modeline offered the buyers of 1970 a unique experience from that of 1950 or 1960.

Arthur Jacobs's 1968 tilt-activated table lamps.
Photographer Libby Danforth

A 1967 Arthur Jacobs–designed chandelier.
Photographer Libby Danforth

A 1967 Arthur Jacobs–designed floor lamp.
Photographer Libby Danforth

Modern lighting is really on the beam at Modeline of California. New 1970 models verge on the spectacular in form, material selection and mechanical ingenuity, as the Los Angeles decorative lamp manufacturer enters its 25th year. Modeline erases any doubts that Modern reflects the trend of the 1970s with a selection of 30 new styles equally at home on Earth or Moon. Acrylic and chrome are the material stars of Modeline's 1970 presentation. The two materials are noteworthy for both the large volume of usage and, more important, the very natural way California stylists Jack Haywood and Arthur Jacobs have made acrylic and chrome an integral part of the new designs. There is nothing forced about the plexiglass shade of a new Haywood desk, table, or boudoir model. Its two-piece shade is pleasingly shaped as no other lampshade material before it. The inventive mind of Haywood, a practicing Los Angeles architect by profession, is demonstrated by the snap-out mechanisms of the acrylic shade, permitting easy bulb changing. The lamp is offered in chrome or flared wood base or as a hanging lamp, and the acrylic comes in either smoke or white tones. Haywood's use of opaque, white acrylic on a modern lamp styled like a grandfather's clock is another design triumph. These come in table or floor models and are meticulously constructed with specially designed counter-sunk fittings, again easily removed for simple bulb replacement. Jacobs' contributions are equally impressive. His use of globes with walnut, black or wet-colored wood finishes has become a trademark. He employs both the Modeliter and Saturn switches, which he invented, most effectively. Polished chrome or brass square tubing appear in many of his new pieces against the softening warmth of woods. That the Age of Modern has returned is reflected at every turn in Modeline's many across-the-country showrooms this winter. Furthermore, the newest efforts are important enough to enhance the firm's reputation for creating more than lamps, but rather "lighted furniture."

—Kathleen Whalen, Los Angeles Times

The Modeline "Cube Lite" boudoir lamp. *Photographer Paige Hood*

Opposite: The Model 8885 acrylic checkerboard table lamp by Arthur Jacobs. *Photographer Paige Hood*

The Arthur Jacobs "Arch," in floor and table lamp varieties. Photographer Paige Hood

Throughout 1970, these "new modern" lamps continued to gain traction and change the look of modern lighting both among California lamp makers and throughout the rest of the country. Now, with the advent of a new decade, there was sufficient sales data to predict future buying trends. Confident that these futuristic modern designs would continue their upward sales trajectory, Bernie and Jack put their heads together on a name for this line. "California Contemporary," a name that originated with Jerry Bertram of Sherman-Bertram Furniture, had a nice ring to it and seemed to encapsulate the unique, West Coast feel of these lamps. With Bertram's blessing, Modeline began to capitalize on this—both as a name for these space-age lamps and as an idea. The space-age look, after all, directly represented what California furniture and lamp manufacturing was all about. Whereas modernism makes "no concession to traditional motifs," California modernism went even further. In simple, raw terms, California is the geographical end to the lower, contiguous United States. In American culture, California tended to occupy the cutting edge of ideas. In lighting design, where California went, the rest of the United States would follow. So it was only fitting that as the new visual stimuli of outer space were introduced, California Contemporary would be the Modeline grouping to represent this new era in the form of interior lighting.

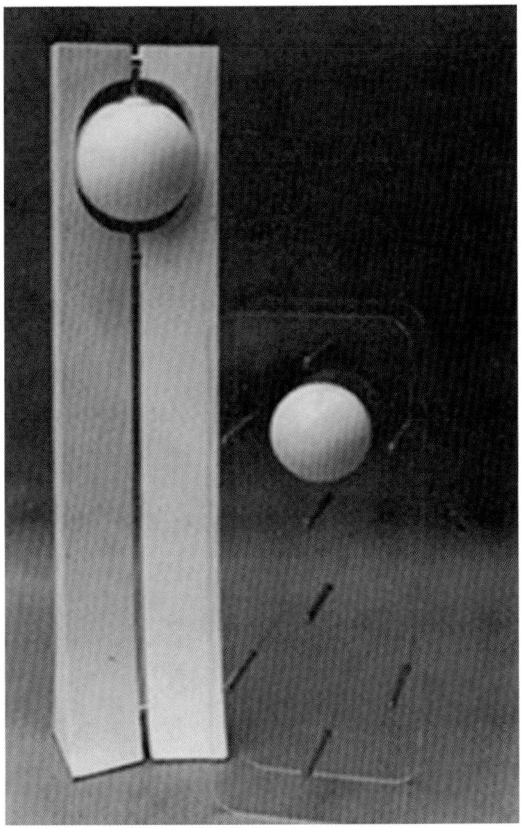

California Contemporary swept the country. The lighting firms that could not quickly adapt to this new style slipped, one after another, into extinction. All the while, Modeline of California lit the way for all other brands that chose to follow. For all the unknown elements of the future, there was one fact that had become abundantly clear—the 1970s belonged to Jack Haywood. Haywood's futurist contributions to the California Contemporary line became only more cutting edge as the decade progressed. Using his 1969 and 1970 success as a springboard, he, along with Arthur Jacobs, Bill Dorff, and Mark Stehrenberger, conceived a series of designs that they believed would make a monumental splash in the design world. These designs, if well received, would change the look of Modeline once and for all. These new concepts returned to the all-wood tradition, but in a ground-up reimagining of what that meant. They comprised wood frames with bent plywood shells and, either when finished in a transparent toner or a wet-look opaque polyester, presented as the most futuristic offering at any lighting firm in the world. A trial run of twenty-four models in this style debuted at showrooms across the United States in the spring of 1971, and hardly a word of criticism could be heard. One of Haywood's designs won the 1971 California Design Eleven award for design excellence, and the same model was selected for the "What's New in the U.S.A." exhibition in Berlin later that year.

Jack Haywood's award-winning floor lamp design (*on the left*). *Copyright Modeline Co.*

With all the attention that California Contemporary was receiving, it took very little convincing for John Keal to give the green light to the design team to continue creating these bent-wood designs. Jack Haywood, who at this point had been with Modeline for nearly fifteen years, had historically been just a bit too ahead of his time. Unlike the other designers, Haywood's designs had the unusual distinction of generally not experiencing significant sales until sometimes years after their initial release. This was no longer the case. It took the culture embracing a look of the future for Jack Haywood's designs to finally make sense. Haywood wasted no time in seizing the opportunity to gain the long-overdue recognition that had been enjoyed by Arthur Jacobs and John Keal for many years. In early 1972, Jack Haywood led the design of more than two hundred California Contemporary lamps set for release in the fall of that year.

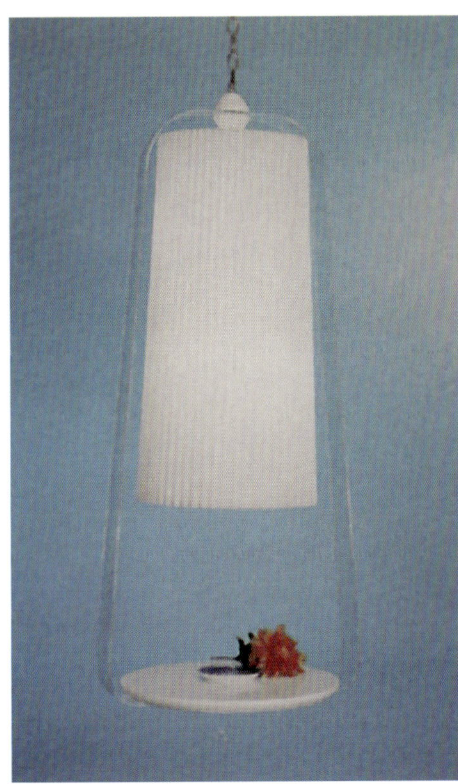

Copyright Modeline Co.

Copyright Modeline Co.

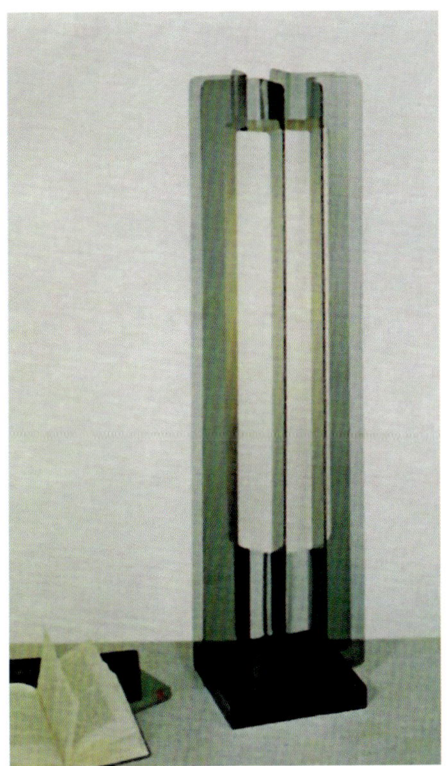

Copyright Modeline Co.

Copyright Modeline Co.

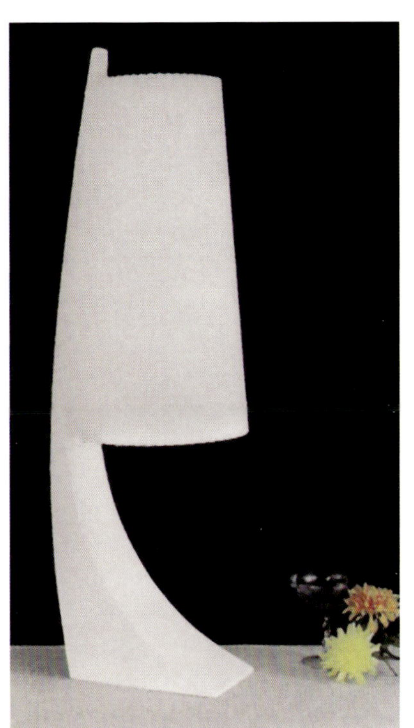

Copyright Modeline Co.

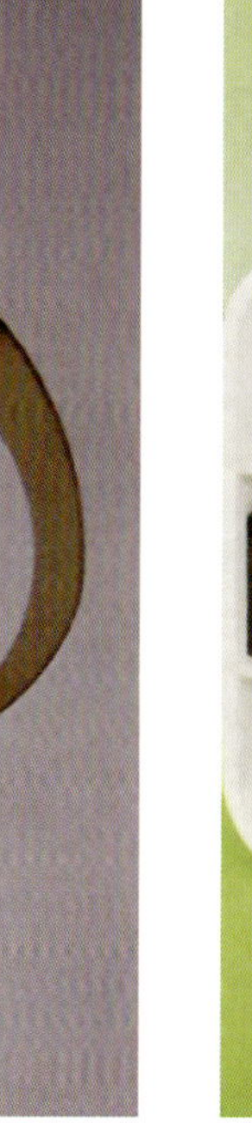

Copyright Modeline Co.

Copyright Modeline Co.

Copyright Modeline Co.

An Arthur Jacobs–designed California Contemporary floor lamp. *Photographer Paige Hood*

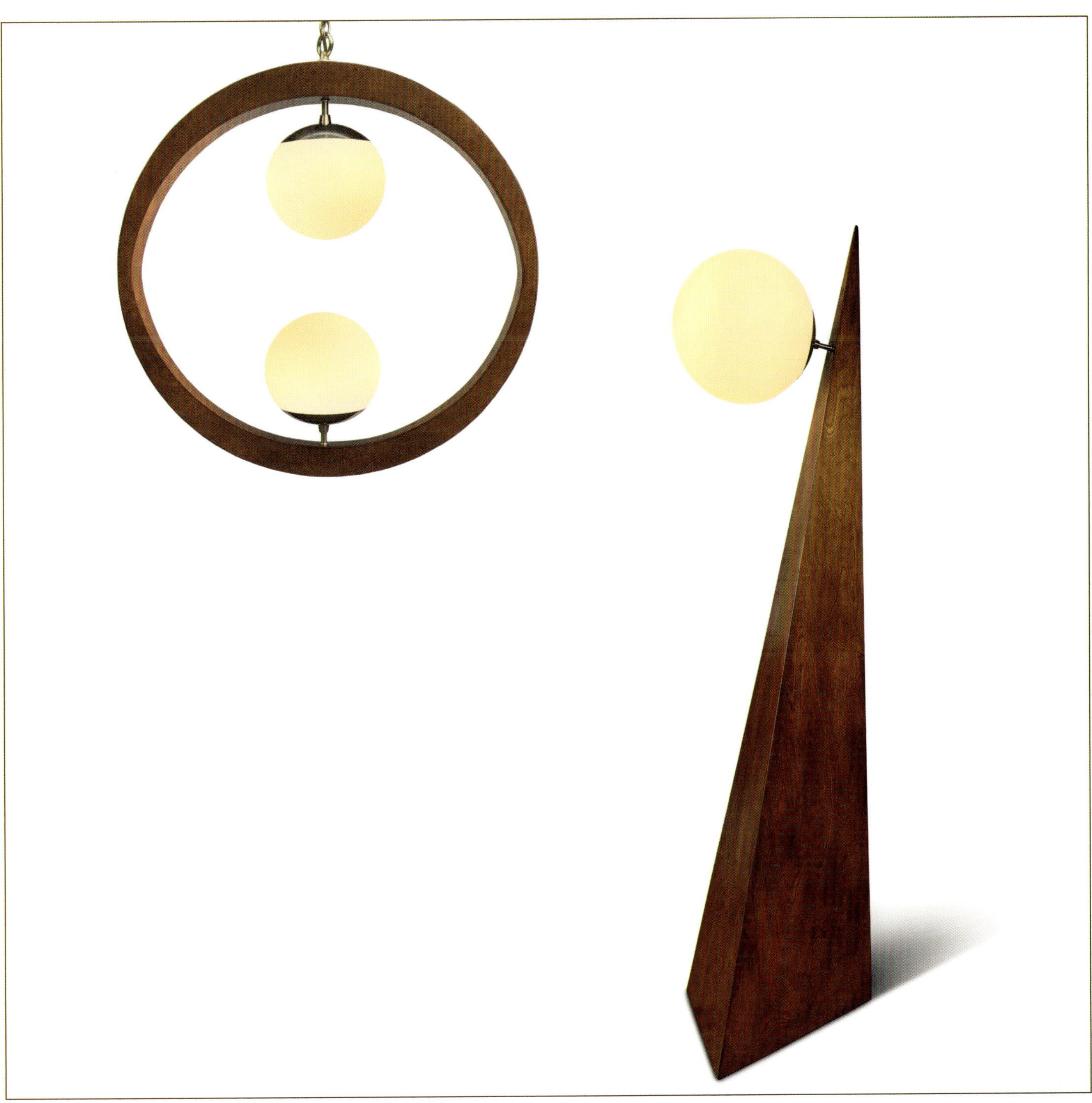

An Arthur Jacobs-designed California Contemporary chain lamp and a Jack Haywood-designed California Contemporary floor lamp

Opposite: A Jack Haywood–designed California Contemporary floor lamp. *Photographer Paige Hood*

A Jack Haywood–designed California Contemporary room divider. *Photographer Paige Hood*

A Jack Haywood–designed California Contemporary hanging occasional table.
Photographer Paige Hood

A Jack Haywood–designed California Contemporary chain lamp. *Photographer Paige Hood*

A Jack Haywood–designed California Contemporary floor lamp. *Photographer Paige Hood*

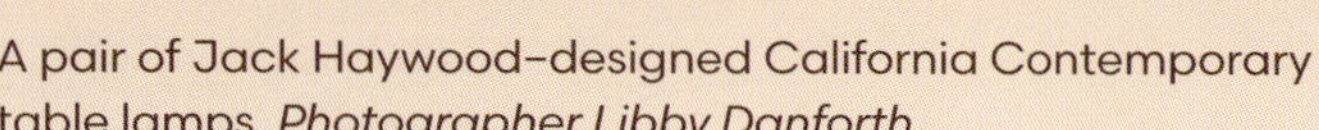

A pair of Jack Haywood–designed California Contemporary table lamps. *Photographer Libby Danforth*

An Arthur Jacobs–designed California Contemporary chandelier. *Photographer Libby Danforth*

An Arthur Jacobs–designed California Contemporary chandelier. *Photographer Libby Danforth*

The sales of the California Contemporary lamps carried Modeline through the end of 1974. By the beginning of 1975, however, sales at Modeline began to slow. With Arthur Jacobs preparing for retirement and Jack Haywood dedicating more of his time to commercial architecture, nothing had been prepared to succeed California Contemporary. John Keal led the team in creating a short-lived line called "Country Western," which consisted of forty table and floor lamps made from

A Mark Stehrenberger–designed California Contemporary table lamp. *Courtesy of Mark Stehrenberger*

Mark Stehrenberger's son posing with one of his father's California Contemporary designs. *Courtesy of Mark Stehrenberger*

Sequoia, designed in an early American space-age blended style. These lamps performed poorly and were retired within a year. While there would never have been a time at which laying down his life's work felt right, California Contemporary seemed to Bernie to be the most appropriate finale to his time with Modeline. At sixty-seven years old, having had a career that took him from being a publicly shamed and unemployed Communist to being one of the most influential executives in the furniture industry, Bernie began to explore the possibility of retirement. His decision to sell Modeline was complicated by the fact that the company had slipped into a relatively serious lull in sales. If sales were to decline any further, the brand would become quite unappealing to most buyers. Returning to the man whose guidance had carried Modeline through every difficult transition, Bernie consulted Percy Solotoy. Percy, who had retired from Brown-Saltman several years before this point, offered to shop the company around to his friends and colleagues. Bernie took a serious interest in ensuring that Modeline would remain in the hands of someone who would care for the firm, and he trusted Percy to take this into consideration.

CHAPTER 9

The End of an Era

Percy Solotoy. *Copyright Modeline Co.*

I'd like to tell you where [the furniture industry] is going, because I really think I know. Two years ago, I sat in on the first all-industry conference in San Francisco. For three days I listened to outsiders–people not in the furniture business–tell us what they found wrong with it and what we should do. I came away very depressed because everything they said was true and I couldn't see myself, as a small manufacturer, fitting into what they were talking about. Two years have gone by, I've had a lot of time to think about this, and I still feel the same way.

This is what they told us: First, the furniture industry is an archaic industry in the sense that we are still doing business like our grandfathers. We are a Papa-and-Mama grocery store operation. And they told us, "Gentlemen, those of you who think you can go on doing business this way ought to get your money out of it and do something else. Because very soon now something big is going to come along and run right over you, and you're going to be smashed into the ground." And what is that something? Nobody has to remind you that there's something happening called merging. And the pace is accelerating. These mergers are not furniture manufacturing companies in the old sense. They are conglomerates of all kinds of industries. This is how it will happen. First, people in the business will merge with each other. There's been enough of this now that the really big conglomerates are starting to take a healthy look at us and find a brand new, unmined field. And once they move in, the furniture business becomes a different kind of business, not only on the manufacturing but on the retail level. Then designing is going to become a completely different game. Look at the auto business. Ford and General Motors and Chrysler, the Big Three, are not concerned with their dealers at all. . . . Whatever you may think of their designs, they are very well attuned to what they think is a market. And they are attuned directly, not by way of all the filtering things that go on in the furniture business. If I want to learn what the consumer wants and ask 10 of my dealers, I get 10 different answers. The auto people can make a design go because they go directly to the consumer with it . . . they have the money, the energy. the brains, the whole bit to go directly to the consumer with the product. The dealer merely operates as a vehicle through which this flows. It's a convenience for General Motors to do it this way, and when it stops being a convenience, I suppose they'll sell direct. Now, I'm not suggesting that this a good or a bad thing. But I do want to point out that the large manufacturer has more money to spend when it comes to the developmental aspects of our business. I think it's much simpler for Drexel to experiment with a new type of plastic or of automated manufacturing than it is for Brown-Saltman. They'll spend up to a million dollars and can easily justify that.

It's not true that everybody who's small is going to disappear. There will survive some very small manufacturers who are specialists, who are design-committed, innovators, creative artists. They will be able to survive because they need only this little bit to survive on. But it also means that if a creative thing requires enormous production facilities to come about, then it can't be.

–Percy Solotoy, 1968

In the late 1960s, Brown-Saltman had fallen on difficult times. The firm was not able to adapt quickly enough to the changes brought by the end of the decade, and sales entered a freefall. Solotoy was well aware of his own limitations. Believing that he had exhausted his available resources in turning the company back toward profitability, he sought an individual who could bring a fresh set of eyes to the struggling firm. The gentleman who was ultimately able to turn things around for Percy was David Fields. Like Percy, David had lived quite a fascinating life. He spent several years in the mid-1960s working in advertising in New York, enjoying a fair amount of success in this difficult and competitive field. Through his work in advertising, he was noticed by President Richard Nixon's chief of staff, Bob Haldeman. Haldeman gave David a job, and he relocated to California. David spent several years working for Haldeman, eventually resigning in the early 1970s when the climate surrounding Nixon became untenable. Fields was preparing to move back to New York when he was contacted by a headhunter who presented a unique proposition. He was told that Percy Solotoy of Brown-Saltman was looking for a talented individual who was skilled in marketing to come work for him and help build the brand back up to its former glory. In exchange for these services, he would be given a salary as well as equity in the firm. David took this job, and Percy became David Fields's friend and mentor. David worked hard to absorb all the information that he could about the case goods industry and what made one brand more successful than another. This education was quite effective, and David was ultimately successful in breathing life back into Brown-Saltman. When the time came for Percy Solotoy to retire, David assumed the position of president of the company. David's skill set was a perfect match for Modeline of California, so naturally, he was the first person whom Percy contacted about purchasing the company. David initially declined, feeling that his hands were too full to take on another project. Later the same year, David sold Brown-Saltman to a pair of businessmen named William Chan and Bob Fogerty. The two gentlemen had purchased several other furniture manufacturers before this, and David insisted that the sale of Brown-Saltman was contingent on him assuming the role of president of their furniture division. After this sale, David went on to negotiate a long list of furniture maker acquisitions for Chan and Fogerty, including Dux, Pennsylvania House, Kittinger, Dunbar, and others. This string of acquisitions ended in an upstream merger with General Mills, which created a considerable amount of personal wealth for David. At this point, in 1976, Percy called David again and asked if he would take another look at Modeline. David did take a look and was not impressed with the financials. Modeline had dwindled down to a mere $40,000 in monthly sales by this point.

Percy suggested to David that he acquire Modeline personally rather than for Chan and Fogerty, since the company could be purchased at a price that was not out of reach for David. With a bit of hesitation, David agreed to meet with Bernie Roberts in the summer of 1976 to negotiate the purchase of the company. In the years leading up to this, David had sat in more of these meetings than most executives had in a lifetime. Rarely did they stray far from a certain script. The price was agreed upon, a bit of fine print was discussed, lawyers did their talking and then a handshake, and that was the end. So it came as a surprise when David arrived with his lawyer to see Bernie Roberts with his lawyer, Esther, and Shirley. The abnormalities did not stop there. The negotiations were long and chaotic. David's lawyer asked Bernie's lawyer a question, only to be interrupted by Bernie, only for Bernie to be interrupted by Esther, who was interrupted by Shirley, as they all began to talk over each other. This went on for over an hour until Bernie's lawyer shouted them all down and said that if some kind of order could not be maintained, he would leave the meeting. David was not accustomed to buying a firm directly from its founder, and certainly never from an individual as passionately invested as Bernie Roberts. What became of Modeline was of monumental concern to the Robertses, since it had been their entire lives for thirty years. In the end, a deal was reached. David Fields shook each of their hands, the Robertses packed their personal effects into the car, and, for the last time in their lives, they drove away from the Beaudry Avenue factory.

The inventive mind of California architect-designer Martin Borenstein has created a system of lighting furniture for Modeline of California that he describes as expressing many moods and faces. Known as Discovery Collection I, the system is ingenious in that the few elements that make up the collection, when placed in various combinations, form hundreds of different lamps and lighting effects. The primary design is pure sculpture. A soaring walnut wood standard that revolves on a solid black wooden base. This standard is put to an unlimited number of beautiful lighting furniture uses as floor lamps or table lamps. as Illuminated shelving for art objects or as vanities. The standard can be revolved 360 degrees so that light can be directed where desired and the dimmer control switch regulates intensity from strong to mood lighting. Borenstein achieves further flexibility by using three different lighting constructions on the standards (a single sphere held by a graceful rod, three in-line spheres, or a handsome metal shell covered by an acrylic shade). The reflective shell is handsome alone on a floor, as a table or chair lamp. But it really comes into its own when used in clusters as a hanging lamp or fixture. The shells pivot outward or inward for direct or indirect lighting. The position changes not only adjust the light, but also give a different look in style and scale to the fixture. The net result is that the Discovery Collection provides an opportunity for lighting lovers to form as many clusters and combinations of lamps as their imagination will allow, knowing that the sculpture-like quality is equally pleasing whether lighted or not.

—*Los Angeles Times*, 1977

Having worked so closely with Bernie for so long, Arthur Jacobs and Jack Haywood did not continue working at Modeline after the sale. David had his brother Jerry do a bit of design work for the firm while he got to work on finding the Arthur Jacobs and Jack Haywood of the late 1970s. He was well positioned to secure such talent, since he had worked with some of the most skilled designers in the business while working as president of the contemporary products group for General Mills. Two of the designers with whom he had worked in the past, Martin Borenstein and Charles Gibilterra, happily agreed to do design work for David. Both men were fans of Modeline, and Borenstein had worked with Bernie Roberts in the past. Borenstein was first to return with a line that he called the Discovery Collection I.

A Martin Borenstein–designed Discovery Collection I lighted shelf. *Copyright Modeline Co.*

The Discovery Collection I did increase sales at Modeline, as well as give the firm a bit of much-needed publicity. David Fields's Modeline did not experience serious success, though, until Charles Gibilterra presented his designs. Charles worked closely with David to develop a line of lamps that would do justice to Modeline's heritage while also contributing something unique from the current or past offerings. What he arrived at, comprising eleven unique table, floor, and chain lamps, was a line called California Cactus. These charming cactus lamps were constructed from blue, wormy ponderosa pine that Modeline purchased from Brooks-Scanlon of Oregon, finished in Watco Danish oil. Each arm of the cactus lamp was capped with a glass cloche shade, clearly displaying the dimmable Edison bulbs. Little artistic liberty was taken in representing the form of a saguaro cactus, but this new lamp accomplished precisely what it was designed to accomplish. The wholly wooden base stayed true to the spirit of Modeline, and the biomorphic design played the same tune that Arthur Jacobs's Model 350 had in 1956. For the last time, Modeline of California demonstrated that the motifs of the natural world would forever be fashionable.

Modeline of California has combined the natural beauty of ancient trees with the visual appeal of cactus to achieve the most unique statement in fashion lighting in recent years, California Cactus. Towering Ponderosa Pine stained blue from mineral absorption and riddled by four species of nature's own artisans, the wood beetle, provide a lumber for these lamps of unusual character. The application of clear oil as a finish, highlighted by crystal glass domes[,] result in lighting unlike anything else in the world, sure to become a conversation piece in any fashionable home. Modeline's lamps are intended to be of enduring appeal. The uniqueness of California Cactus fulfills that objective. Each of the 11 lamps in the collection was conceived by Charles Gibilterra, noted California Designer.

–*Desert Sun*, 1977

Charles Gibilterra. *Courtesy of Charles Gibilterra*

A Charles Gibilterra–designed California Cactus floor lamp. *Photographer Michelle Seal*

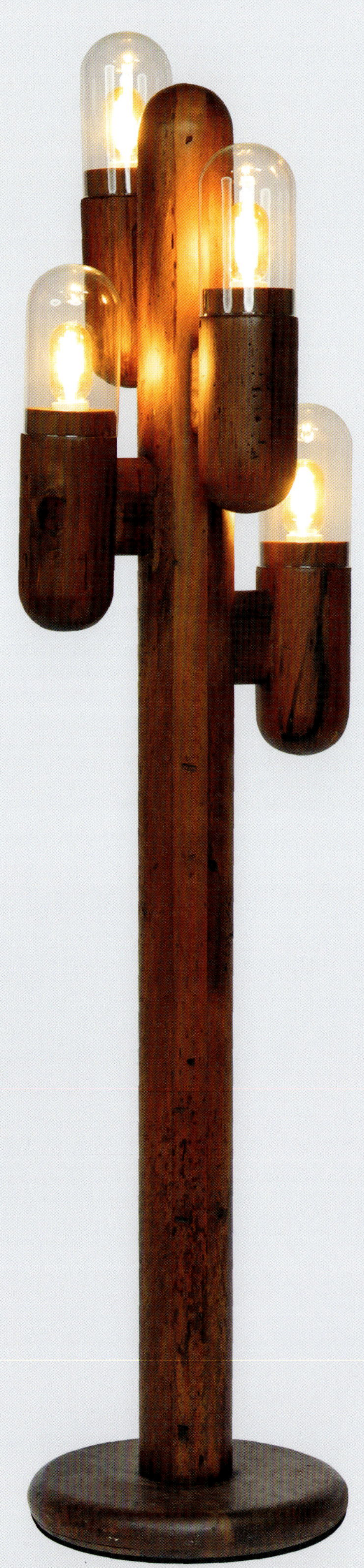

A Charles Gibilterra–designed California Cactus chain lamp. *Photographer Paige Hood*

When the time came to officially unveil California Cactus to the public at San Francisco Furniture Mart's Summer Market in 1977, nearly half a million dollars of orders flooded in within four days' time. For a company that had dwindled down to a mere $40,000 in monthly sales, this was monumental. Buyers loved the California Cactus, and in short order it brought Modeline up to a 3.5-million-dollar revenue. The renewed buzz at Modeline attracted one of its founding fathers to rejoin the firm. John Keal, who had not been very active since leaving Modeline a few years prior, bought 12 percent equity in the company. His role, like his time with Bernie, would be to assist David in selecting designs and guiding the designers in creating new, cohesive models.

David Fields traveled the country, opening up Levitz, Strouss, Marshall Field's, Bloomingdale's, and virtually all other high-end department stores to this new line. Wherever the Cactus went, torrential sales followed. So when the time came in 1978 to create the successor to the Cactus, David went right back to Charles Gibilterra. Charles created another rustic line that he called Honey Oak. Honey Oak was a collection of twenty-four lamps that had an appearance similar to the Cactus but with a slightly more space-age influence. They were constructed from red oak, were topped with spherical glass globes, and had a similar, natural-finished appearance to the Cactus. David was eager to continue the momentum that the California Cactus had created, so he came up with a creative way to incentivize his nine national salesmen to push this new line. David offered a bonus of $1 per lamp sold to whoever sold the most single lamps on opening day of San Francisco Furniture Mart's Summer Market in 1979. Over $600,000 in orders were booked on that single day. The next day, David delivered the bonus in the form of a massive bag of Susan B. Anthony silver dollars. This was quite a sight to behold and served as equally comedic and motivating to these salesmen. The momentum of Honey Oak and California Cactus continued through the year, bringing Modeline of California up to $5 million in yearly sales by the end of 1979. There was hardly a department store or furniture shop in the country that didn't want a piece of this action.

A 1978 John Keal–designed lighted etagere. *Copyright Modeline Co.*

Opposite: A Charles Gibilterra–designed Honey Oak table lamp. *Photographer Libby Danforth*

A Charles Gibilterra–designed California Cactus floor lamp.
Courtesy of Charles Gibilterra

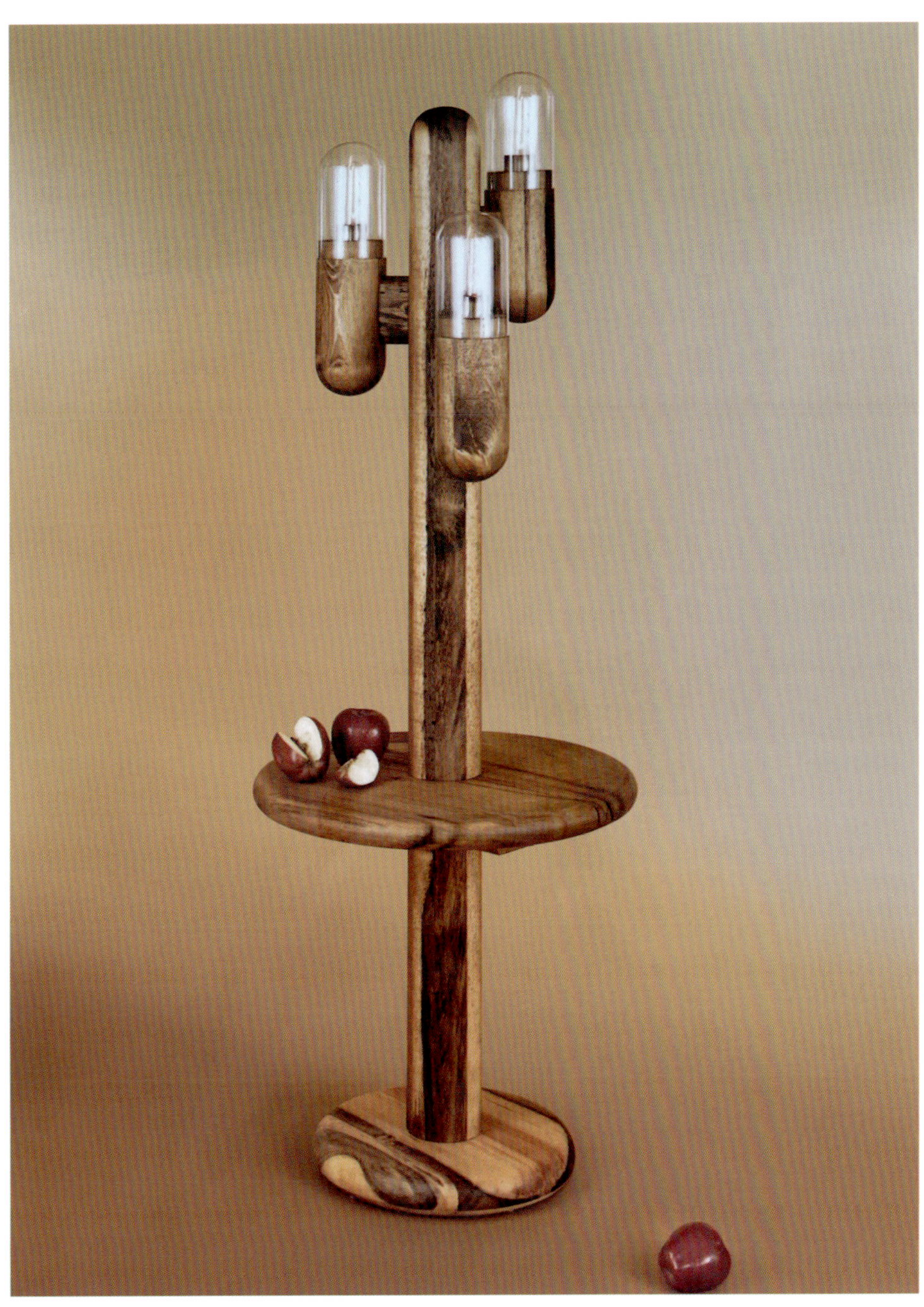

A Charles Gibilterra–designed California Cactus occasional table floor lamp. *Courtesy of Charles Gibilterra*

A Charles Gibilterra–designed California Cactus table lamp.
Courtesy of Charles Gibilterra

A Charles Gibilterra–designed Honey Oak floor and table lamp.
Courtesy of Charles Gibilterra

A Charles Gibilterra–designed Honey Oak table lamp.
Courtesy of Charles Gibilterra

A Charles Gibilterra–designed Honey Oak chandelier.
Courtesy of Charles Gibilterra

A Charles Gibilterra-designed Honey Oak chandelier.
Courtesy of Charles Gibilterra

A Charles Gibilterra–designed table and floor lamp.
Courtesy of Charles Gibilterra

A Charles Gibilterra–designed floor and table lamp.
Courtesy of Charles Gibilterra

A Charles Gibilterra–designed table lamp and occasional table floor lamp.
Courtesy of Charles Gibilterra

Above: A Charles Gibilterra–designed table and floor lamp. *Courtesy of Charles Gibilterra*

A Charles Gibilterra–designed table and floor lamp. *Courtesy of Charles Gibilterra*

It was at this moment, during the peak of what appeared to be the renaissance of Modeline, that the company became an unruly child for David Fields. One afternoon in 1979 was greeted by calamity when two immigration control vehicles pulled up and parked outside the Modeline plant. With tools and materials falling to the ground, employees rushed out of rear exit doors and windows. The overwhelmed plant supervisor struggled to restore order as he realized that he had failed to effectively communicate that the production crew for *Charlie's Angels* would be arriving that day to film an episode at the plant. The prop immigration trucks posed no genuine threat. Sadly, this moment of chaos would serve as a mere dress rehearsal for Modeline's late 1970s factory woes. The death of Modeline came in a rapid succession of punches. The first of these ultimately fatal blows was thrown, albeit inadvertently, by Muhammad Ali.

The Modeline plant, which had not moved from the North Beaudry Avenue location since 1948, shared a wall with another factory that had been occupied by Nobilium Restorations until 1978. Modeline's new neighbor was a memorabilia plant that was owned by Muhammad Ali. As Ali retired from his boxing career, he began spending more time around his plant, where he met David Fields. Ali and Fields became friends. The two often began their days together with coffee and exchanging stories at the Modeline office or convening later in the afternoon for lunch at Carney's on Sunset Boulevard.

Things at the plant were moving along swimmingly until, one night in 1979, David received a frantic phone call from his plant supervisor. The main waterline in Muhammad Ali's plant had burst and flooded the Modeline factory with 3 feet of water. Nearly all inventory, supplies, and tools were damaged to a point of total loss. This resulted in a months-long legal battle with David's insurance company. The insurance company ultimately agreed to cover the entire expense of reconstruction, to be paid out in monthly increments over the course of two years. By the time that David had reached this agreement, the backlog at Modeline had grown to a nearly impossible amount. While most of the focus was placed on fulfilling backlogged orders, David began approaching new designers in hopes that another sales boom could help bail Modeline out of this mess. Kipp Stewart and Stewart MacDougall designed a line of table lamps and lighted pedestals that would have been much more at home among

Copyright Modeline Co.

A Kipp Stewart–designed pair of lighted plant stands.
Photographer Libby Danforth

the Arthur Jacobs–era offerings than with the Gibilterra-dominated late 1970s lamps. Sculpted from walnut and oak and some adorned with hanging jewels, the lamps bore no resemblance to the direction that Modeline had gone over the past few years. These lamps crashed without leaving the runway, seeing only minimal sales before it became clear that no amount of advertising could convince buyers that these were the lamps suited for the interiors of 1980.

The sales of the California Cactus and Honey Oak lines were keeping Modeline afloat, but not by a significant margin at this point and to no benefit to Gibilterra. With resources redirected to cover repairs to the factory, royalty payments came to a halt. This made securing new design talent impossible. Even after the factory recovered from the flood, the lost time and revenue set in motion a series of events from which Modeline could not recover. To fulfill as many back orders as possible to restore faith among Modeline's clients, David added a second and third factory shift. This well-intentioned decision ultimately cost Modeline more money than it generated. One night, a factory employee was working while under the influence of narcotics, and he reached up into a planer to check its operation. That careless decision cost this individual a considerable portion of his right hand and earned David Fields an uncomfortable interaction with the California Occupational Safety and Health Administration. When the OSHA representative visited the plant, David's demeanor was about what one might expect from an executive who was dealing with the comedy of errors that Modeline had become—a bit flippant and short on patience. Upon meeting this representative, David informed him that his visit was an unnecessary waste of both of their time, since the plant had recently been rebuilt due to the flood. The representative then pointed to a loose wall covering and told David that it would be a $10,000 fine. This moment sobered David up, but the fines did not end there.

Two weeks after this visit, David received a certified letter from OSHA notifying him of a total of $110,000 in fines. David paid a visit to the regional manager of OSHA in a desperate attempt to reduce the fine. "I can't pay this fine," David explained to him. "It's ill-deserved, and we have been limping along since our great flood. If you insist that I pay this, I'll close the plant, and you'll put seventy-eight hardworking people in the heart of Los Angeles out of work." "You wouldn't really do that," he replied. "You want to bet? Check my record. Part of my job with General Mills as a group president was shutting down unprofitable plants." The OSHA representative was skeptical, sarcastically asking David Fields if he was the Dark Knight. "No, I'm simply telling you that I cannot pay you $110,000. It is an ill-deserved punishment for minor infractions. I *will* close the plant." OSHA ultimately reduced the fine to $10,000, David wrote them a check, and this close brush with Modeline's bankruptcy was behind him. No sooner was this episode finished than the wood-chipper exhaust fan at Modeline caught fire, resulting in the plant being shut down for nearly two months.

At this point, David met with his attorney. He vented his frustrations and asked for input on what the correct course of action might be. The money was flowing in as long as the factory was operational, but one thing after another was preventing this. David had never run a plant this old except for Dunbar, but Dunbar's facility was considerably more updated than Modeline's. His attorney suggested that it might be time to get out of the business, but David did not want to end on a sour note. He felt a duty to the workers at the plant to exhaust every possible option to restore Modeline. It was about this time, early in 1981, that the phone calls started coming in. First, from the president of Levitz. "I'm afraid that we cannot pay you the $400,000 that we owe," he began. "Worse yet, I'm going to have to ship all of the merchandise back to you and bill you for the freight." This may have been survivable for Modeline if not for the tsunami of canceled orders that followed. One after another, dealers and department stores ended all future business.

Just like that, the recession of 1981 swept in and extinguished the last bit of light at Modeline of California.

It was clear that Modeline was not prepared to weather this storm. David pumped as much of his own money into the company as possible for the sake of the employees, who, at this point, were well aware of the situation. There was no sign that this economic downturn would blow over quickly, and it simply ceased making any sense to throw good money after bad. Ultimately, David's lender—Walter E. Heller & Company—called to say that they were getting out of the durable-goods business. David was given an opportunity to pay them back, but there would be no future advances on accounts receivable, and he would henceforth no longer be considered a client, along with twenty-six other furniture manufacturers in Los Angeles.

On December 15, 1981, an orderly auction was held by Max Rouse & Sons that sold off all the tools, inventory, and materials. After thirty-five years in business, the doors at the Beaudry Avenue plant were closed forever.

CHAPTER 10

The Legacy of Modeline of California

Lamp sketches by Delaney Smith

After retiring from both Modeline of California and Prudential in 1976, Arthur Jacobs returned to his first love—the natural world. Arthur and Peggy Jacobs purchased a 5-acre avocado, lemon, and lime farm in Fallbrook, California, which Arthur tended in the early part of his retirement. During this period, Arthur spent his Tuesdays flying radio-controlled airplanes and many weekends fly-fishing. Jacobs lived long enough to see the beginning of the resurgence in popularity of Modeline lamps. When his youngest son was selling him on the merits of computers and Google, to which Arthur had a strong aversion, he plugged "Modeline of California" into the search engine to show his father what had become of his lamps. Upon seeing pages of collectors and dealers singing the praises of what they called "midcentury modern" (a phrase that was new to Arthur), he was left unmoved and unimpressed with the internet. Arthur passed away in 2016 at the age of ninety. His family remembers him fondly, and, to this day, his sons are known to sometimes pause when entering a building to look up at the ceiling lights as a way of paying homage to the father of modern lighting.

Jack Haywood dedicated his full efforts to building his architecture firm after he left Modeline. He experienced a few close brushes with success but generally struggled to get work. The work that he did get was often artistically unfulfilling and low paying. By the end of his career, he did manage to leave his mark, having been project architect on buildings in seventeen states. Many of these projects, though, were

convenience stores and fast-food restaurants, which was a point of frustration for Haywood. Outside of these, he designed buildings for Bank of America, Lloyds Bank California, and several community buildings for Los Angeles Parks and Recreation. One of his proudest contributions to Los Angeles architecture came in 1984, when he codesigned the first state-funded African American museum in the country—the California African American Museum. He continued to nurse this firm along until the late 1980s, when he decided to try his hand at residential design. He bought a plot of land in the Hollywood Hills and began construction on what he hoped would become his greatest creation. This undertaking quickly became much more costly than Jack had anticipated. He was unable to pay back the loan that he had taken to complete this project, and the property was seized and sold and the work he had completed was demolished. Haywood never recovered from this. His mental, physical, and financial well-being declined steadily until he died from a heart attack in 1997. Jack spent his life dreaming up objects that did not yet exist. This imaginative spirit lives on in his son Gar, who is an award-winning fiction writer.

John Keal went into semiretirement after Modeline closed in 1981, and split his time between his Los Angeles home and Honolulu condo. He continued to sketch designs well into his old age, but in a sad turn of events for a man whose greatest asset was an unmatched eye, he developed macular degeneration. This prevented him from continuing his work to any meaningful capacity, and it contributed to his accidentally setting fire to his office. This resulted in the destruction of most of his original design sketches. As his health declined, he was cared for by his daughter in Hawaii, where he passed away in 1999.

Bernie and Esther split their time between Twentynine Palms and Los Angeles. The two initially enjoyed retirement and spent much of their time involved in various political and philanthropic engagements. Although they never again worked in the field of lighting, the two maintained a close relationship with Percy Solotoy and took an active interest in the goings-on at Modeline and other Los Angeles firms. In 1984, Esther was diagnosed with lung cancer, which took a massive toll on the Roberts family. Bernie and Shirley cared for her until she succumbed to the disease in 1987. The loss of his wife, with whom he had traversed all the great successes and struggles at Modeline, devastated Bernie. Modeline was, after all, something of a love letter from Bernie to Esther, and Bernie imbued the brand with all the characteristics that he saw in her—beauty, mystery, and sophistication. Grieving her loss, Bernie found himself in a period of identity crisis. He struggled with the idea that the significance of his contribution to modern lighting had been forgotten, and that he had been passed by the changing tastes of American consumers. Now, without the one with whom he had shared it all, he viewed himself as a man without a place in the world. Around this time, Bernie's friend and colleague Jerry Bertram encouraged him to channel some of his heartbreak into philanthropy. Bertram had been active for a number of years in donating furniture to the Synanon organization. Viewed through the lens of history, it would be all too easy to question the wisdom in this decision. There is little doubt, though, that Bertram believed himself to be engaged in a genuinely altruistic endeavor, and he invited Bernie to participate. Through Bernie's subsequent donations of time and money, he became aware of a community in Badger, California, created by Synanon for people in their old age. It was designed to be a multireligious, multiracial community of individuals whose contributions to society would be respected and used to inspire the younger members of this California commune. Six months after Esther's death, Bernie sold and donated his personal belongings and moved into Synanon, where he met Jane Calhoun. Jane had moved in after the death of her sister, and the two bonded quickly. This friendship grew into a romance, and the two were married in 1988. With Synanon coming under heavy scrutiny for the persistent extremism and violence within pockets of the organization, Jane and Bernie left and moved into a retirement village in Palm Desert, California. Although Modeline had nearly been forgotten by the late 1980s, Bernie was ultimately able to make peace with the way that his life played out. In his old age, he found himself looking back on his work with Modeline proudly and would share stories of his experiences with all who would listen. He died of a stroke in 1992 at the age of eighty-four. As of my writing this, a Modeline chandelier still hangs in the home that Bernie and Esther once shared.

After the sale of Modeline, Shirley carried the torch of her father's political and philosophical passions, working both in an occupational and volunteer capacity for a long list of California politicians and civic leaders. Her life was consumed with a commitment to bettering the lives of the working class, minority groups, and the unhoused. In fact, there was hardly a democratic cause in Los Angeles from 1951 until 2010 in which Shirley was not at the center. As the cost of living rose in her community of West Hollywood, she was at the heart of the movement to incorporate West Hollywood so as to allow it to better serve its lower-income residents.

Working under Los Angeles mayor Tom Bradley, she undertook the project of improving accessibility for senior citizens, as well as pushing Bradley to effect as much change as he could in the affordability of healthcare. She was an active member of the Women's Political Committee and the Feminist Majority Foundation, as well as the vice president of the Jewish Labor Committee. Shirley struggled to understand her father's decision to leave Los Angeles but loved and missed her parents deeply and often told stories of her time with them at Modeline in her old age. Shirley succumbed to lung cancer in 2010. She passed away surrounded both by family and nearly every progressive political figure in Los Angeles lining the hall outside her room at Cedars-Sinai hospital. The morning of her passing, she received a letter from President Barack Obama commending her on a life dedicated to the service of others. Shirley was never married and had no children, but she was often seen out on the town in her younger years with Sandy Koufax.

Shirley Roberts never, ever stopped fighting for the things she knew were right and she extended her compassion and love to nearly every person she met. Whether it was rights for workers, advancement for women, transportation for seniors, or improving health care and conditions for Los Angeles' poor–Shirley put the people and the causes around her before herself. She was unlike any other woman I've ever known.

–California State Assembly Speaker John A. Perez

I had the pleasure of working with Shirley on behalf of those less fortunate in our community. She was a strong soul and an outspoken voice of fairness and decency for working people everywhere. I owe much of where I am today to the lessons of her life.

–United States Secretary of Labor Hilda Solis

Shirley Roberts was an amazing woman. Her commitment to progressive causes was unwavering. She was a friend and supporter of so many elected officials across Southern California. Her influence spanned many generations and extended far beyond West Hollywood.

–West Hollywood mayor John Heilman

Shirley was a force of nature. . . . What I remember about her is that she was so honest about her views. Some people on the left or the right are all about abstract ideas. She was a woman of the heart. She reminded me in many ways of a notion that I read once in a card that said, "What is as important as knowledge?" asked the mind; "Caring and seeing with the heart," answered the soul. She was a woman of soul and heart, a woman of love and passion, and I will remember her fondly till my dying days.

–Los Angeles mayor Antonio Villaraigosa

What is a modern lamp? Different from nearly all styles of design and architecture that preceded it, "modern lighting" meant nearly nothing at all upon its initial conception. A modern lamp was simply one that, in the words of Jack Haywood, "made no concession to traditional motifs." By that definition, a modern lamp could have been anything at all that did not resemble its architectural forebearers. Before Modeline, the application of the word "modern" in the field of lighting was exactly that ambiguous. Among all the competing ideas in the postwar years for what modern was or could have become, it was Modeline of California that ultimately gave meaning to the phrase "modern lighting." A modern lamp is any lamp of minimalist composition that pulls its design inspiration directly from nature. In the twentieth century, in a twenty-five-year span, the world witnessed the destructive power of the atomic bomb and gazed back on our planet from another celestial body for the first time. The response to the events of the twentieth century by designers was modernism as we have come to know it. This era of lighting design, subdivided into the three categories of atomic, modern, and space age, represents our world at the micro- and macrolevels as well as our place in the cosmos. This is, perhaps, the trickery behind the seductive effect of Modeline lamps. They feel familiar, like the wonderful world of lighting more broadly, because they are artistic representations of the world of our periphery brought into focus.

The enduring legacy of Modeline of California can be seen in abundance throughout the products of nearly every present-day modern lighting manufacturer and dealer. From the lighted shelves available at nearly every Walmart in the world and the sculptural, wood chain lamps sold by the thousands on Amazon, to the walnut and brass lamps among the offerings of retailers such as Wayfair and West Elm, the spirit of Modeline is as alive today as it ever was. A modern lighting firm, it seems, cannot expect to be taken seriously without standing on the shoulders of Modeline. Without the persons who made this brand what it is being alive to ask for their thoughts, I am left only to speculate on what their reactions would have been to the abundant and unabashed copies of their work. I must imagine, though, that they would have been proud. In the spirit of contribution over competition, they could have confidently seen that their ideas surrounding the coordination of lighting and furniture became the lens through which many future designers saw their work. The use of lighting as an extension of one's personality and a crucial element in the creation of a cohesive interior did not simply remain a good idea—it became *the* good idea. While it is my opinion that credit to the original designer ought to be given in cases where the design has virtually been replicated, the fact that so many of these copies are currently in production serves as a testament to the timeless beauty and inescapably attractive quality of Modeline's wonderful wooden lamps.

Modeline's influencer marketing was so successful that it continues to bear fruit long after the expiration of the brand. Set decorators' love affair with these lamps is as active today as it was in the late 1950s. *Frasier*, *Mad Men*, *Daisy Jones and the Six*, *Dr. Death*, *The Orville*, *Fallout*, *White House Plumbers*, *True Detective*, *Dave*, *For All Mankind*, *Oppenheimer*, *Severance*, and a long list of other television shows and films display the work of Modeline of California. It is not an exaggeration to say that one can hardly watch a 1950s or 1960s period piece without seeing Modeline's ghost in television and cinema.

Whether one remembers Modeline of California for their more than four thousand unique lamp designs, as the most influential American lighting firm of the twentieth century, as an example of progressive values implemented into business practices far ahead of their time, or simply as a relic from the golden age of Hollywood, there is no doubt that these lamps will continue to inspire, excite, and illuminate far into the future.

Bernie and Esther Roberts, 1946.
Courtesy of Randi Måvestrand

NICK FERRELL *is a collector, restorer, and historian of mid-20th-century lighting whose exhaustive research into the history of 20th-century lighting manufacturers has made him the "expert on call" for hundreds of dealers throughout the United States. As owner of Esthetic Vintage, a company that specializes in twentieth-century designer lighting, he has handled tens of thousands of midcentury modern lamps. Through extensive cataloging of unique patterns and design characteristics, he has developed an unparalleled ability to ascertain a lamp's manufacturer, designer, and period. Midcentury modern lighting collectors throughout the world regard Nick as the foremost expert in this field. He lives in Chattanooga, Tennessee.*